MAN: FALLEN AND FREE

CONTRIBUTORS

The Reverend E. W. Kemp, D.D. (Editor)
Fellow and Chaplain of Exeter College, Oxford

The Reverend A. M. Allchin
Librarian of the Pusey House, Oxford

The Reverend J. A. Baker
Fellow and Chaplian of Corpus Christi College, Oxford

The Reverend F. W. Dillistone, D.D.
Fellow and Chaplain of Oriel College, Oxford

The Reverend J. L. Houlden
Fellow and Chaplain of Trinity College, Oxford

The Reverend D. E. Jenkins
Fellow and Chaplain of The Queen's College, Oxford

The Reverend R. S. Lee, D.PHIL.
Fellow and Chaplain of St. Catherine's College and Chaplain of Nuffield College, Oxford

The Reverend F. H. Maycock
Principal of the Pusey House, Oxford

The Reverend D. W. Allen, Principal of St. Stephen's House, Oxford, took part in most of the discussions but was prevented by other commitments from contributing a chapter to the book.

Man: Fallen and Free

OXFORD ESSAYS
ON
THE CONDITION OF MAN

edited by
E. W. KEMP

HODDER AND STOUGHTON

Printed in Great Britain for Hodder and
Stoughton Limited, St. Paul's House,
Warwick Lane, London, E.C.4, by Cox &
Wyman Limited, London, Fakenham and
Reading.

PREFACE

Early in 1963 the Archbishop of Canterbury invited a group of scholars to spend a day with him at Lambeth in discussion of current thought and writing about Christian faith and morals. Five of us who went from Oxford to that meeting thought that we ought to pursue the discussion further and invited friends at Oxford to join us for this purpose, and with a possible book in view.

We began our meetings by considering some of the issues raised by the then recently published book of the Bishop of Woolwich, *Honest to God*. It appeared to us that many of these found a common source in the doctrine of grace, which concerns the action of God for the healing and perfecting of man. But it is precisely the need for this action of God which is called in question today, and so, as we talked further, it became apparent that we must go behind that doctrine to the condition of man and to an examination of the idea of the Fall and the relation of that to current knowledge about human nature and human origins.

Here a choice had to be made. We had reached the point, usual in such groups, when we had acquired a degree of common outlook on certain problems, a common awareness of certain issues. At the same time it was very obvious that we did not contain among ourselves all the varieties of competence necessary to produce a comprehensive volume on the nature and predicament of man. We were notably deficient in the fields of the biological and social sciences. We had to decide whether to expand our group in ways which would remedy these deficiencies or whether to give our book the more limited aim of setting out what various members of the group, in discussion with others, found to be some significant areas of the problem. We chose the latter course because of the difficulty of bringing new people into a discussion which had already lasted for some time and had already produced a common mind on certain problems. We are, therefore, well aware that our treatment of the subject has gaps, both historical and scientific, but we hope that its lack of comprehensiveness may be compensated by a closer coherence.

We begin with chapters which approach the human condition from three different standpoints. The first considers the modern philosophical discussion of responsibility and freedom, and the second the development of the human personality as understood in modern psychology. The third and fourth chapters concern some insights of modern literature into man's predicament and the vision of man as he might be, for in the poetry of Edwin Muir there are similarities to the tradition of 'original righteousness' which, as is shown elsewhere in this book, has often been a presupposition of speculations about the Fall.

In this way we hope to have exposed as still a problem for men of our time that with which the Biblical writers and theologians of the past have tried to deal in evolving the doctrine of the Fall. Obviously we cannot claim a full understanding of the situation in which we live, nor do we claim a full apprehension of the ways in which the Christian revelation bears upon that situation; but it is our belief that the Christian tradition contains within itself, amidst much that is transitory and dated, perceptions of the truth about the human condition, and how we can respond to it, which are the gift of the Author of our being, provided for our guidance.

We turn, therefore, in the second part of our book to look afresh at some of the more important sections of that tradition, beginning as we must with the Old and New Testaments, and in the first two closely related essays of this part we have tried to give a homogeneous and coherent presentation of insights which the Bible expresses in a wide variety of idioms.

Because Christianity was, during the first formative three centuries, so much a religion of the East Mediterranean lands, and because in the Churches of those lands, since the division of the East and Western Empires in the fifth century, we can see a doctrine largely unaffected by the crises, intellectual and political, which marked the West, we follow the chapters on the Bible by a study of certain aspects of Eastern Christianity which specially illuminate our problem.

The personality and intellect of St. Augustine have so powerfully influenced the Fall doctrine of the West that we have inevitably allotted a chapter to him in which an attempt is made to distinguish between the substance of his theology and his understanding of the tradition in which he desired to express it. Most Western thinking about the Fall, and especially in Protestant circles, is so closely related to Augustinianism by affinity or by reaction that we have thought it helpful to select two of the most widely discussed Protestant writers of this century, Bonhoeffer and Tillich, for comparison in this respect. Here is an obvious point of contact with the early stages of our discussion, for one of the first papers read in our group was a criticism of the treatment of these two writers in *Honest to God*. Our work should not, however, be regarded as in any sense a counterblast or reply to that book, for we gratefully acknowledge the stimulus that it has given to theological discussion. We offer our own book as a contribution to the debate which Dr. Robinson started.

Whitsuntide, 1968.   Eric Kemp.

CONTENTS

ACKNOWLEDGEMENTS

The publishers are grateful to the following for permission to reproduce extracts quoted in this book:

Faber and Faber Ltd. for extracts from Edwin Muir, *Collected Poems 1921–1958*

The Hogarth Press Ltd. for extracts from Edwin Muir, *An Autobiography*

James Nisbet and Company Ltd. for extracts from Paul Tillich, *Systematic Theology*

S.C.M. Press Ltd. for extracts from Dietrich Bonhoeffer, *Letters and Papers from Prison*

1 RESPONSIBILITY, FREEDOM AND THE FALL

Some Lines of Investigation

Is it reasonable to hope, as some criminologists, sociologists and psychologists would encourage us to do, that the time will shortly come when we shall dispense with the notion and practice of the punishment of criminals and operate safely and solely with that of the therapeutic treatment of certain types of social deviants?

It is notorious that any suggestion of this nature is likely to be met with emotional reactions which at any rate claim to be expressing a sense of moral outrage. This reaction comes from a very wide range of people—senior judges, bishops and others concerned with public and private morality, as well as many who claim to be voicing the reactions of the ordinary decent man and woman. A man must be held responsible for the good or evil which he does except in exceptional circumstances. To extend the notion of 'exceptional circumstances' to all who violate the law would seem to be far too uncomfortably subversive of our notions of what it is to be a responsible human being. Indeed it might seem to threaten our notion of responsibility altogether, for where do you draw the line? If a man is not to be liable to punishment for rape then for how long will it be reasonable or possible to maintain that the more 'normal' of us are to be blamed for quarrelling with our wives, being rude to those working under us or performing any act which is held to be socially or individually disagreeable or objectionable?

The criminologists, sociologists and psychologists who promote the raising of such questions about the proper understanding and treatment of criminals react to the above reaction with their own sense of outrage. Such an obscurantist response to the problem of deviant human behaviour as is displayed by judges, bishops, head-masters and 'the ordinary decent man' is a compound of a refusal to face facts and a fear of facing facts. Properly objective and statis-tical studies of criminal and delinquent behaviour can and do produce valid correlations between such patterns of behaviour and various combinations of physical, psychological and social factors in the make-up of the individuals displaying this behaviour. An immense amount of careful and rigorous research needs to be done but the results so far are sufficient to give us reasonably scientific confidence that our study of human behaviour will increasingly permit us to locate the causes of criminal behaviour in physical, psychological and social factors which cannot be said to be the individual's *fault*. This being so it will be neither just nor useful to hold him responsible and liable to punishment. Indeed the cruelty as well as the senselessness of punishment is more and more revealed. The question for any civilised approach must become one of care-fully considered restorative treatment.

Further, developing psychological insights into the nature and dynamics of human motivation make it more and more difficult to assert confidently that a particular man has performed a particular evil act from a straightforward evil will in a manner which clearly merits punishment. In addition to making the concept of responsible evil intention (of *mens rea*) very difficult, psychological insight has revealed very significant things about what lies behind the desire to inflict punishment and behind the 'judgement' that certain conduct merits punishment. A strong case can be made out for maintaining that the feeling of the appropriateness of punishment, the 'intuition' that certain conduct 'merits' punishment, is not an insight into some external or overall standard of fitness and justice. It is rather a pro-jection of the internal psychological life whereby 'normal' men and women express their anxieties and fears concerning their own sup-pressed, and hitherto controlled, anti-social desires in the form of anger, indignation and condemnation against those who actually express such desires in action.

Thus the sense of moral outrage, often emotively expressed, when attempts are made to demonstrate that the notion of criminal responsibility is neither tenable, on a wide and proper view of the facts, nor helpful in readjusting the 'criminal' to society and to himself, is to be attributed not only to ignorance but also to fear. There is the fear of having to face up to and come to terms with the 'criminal' tendencies which are normal (and normally controlled) in all of us if the punishment of the overt and practising criminal no longer provides us with scapegoats and opportunities of giving forceful expression to our distaste for that of which we disapprove not only in them but also, and more importantly, in ourselves.

I wish, in the first place, to investigate what would be involved in a 'reasonable' approach to reaching a decision on this issue. In considering this we shall come up against some vitally important aspects of the connection between treating people as responsible or potentially responsible and treating them as human beings. I shall then examine whether the considerations which arise in this area can themselves be illuminated by, and throw light upon, the traditional Christian doctrine of the Fall.

Our problem, then, is that criminological studies, drawing on sociology and psychology, have raised very acute problems about responsibility. We are, it would seem likely, faced with one more version of the debate over free will and determinism, but a version which bites particularly deeply into sensitive spots because it is armed to the teeth with observed, organised and correlated data. Is it reasonable to hope (or fear) that this new version of the problem will lead to a resolution of it such that we shall find less and less use for the concept of responsibility?

I shall proceed with the argument on the assumption that our present sociological and psychological studies are, in general, validly conducted. This does not mean that any particular piece of research is sound nor that the present state of studies has clearly and firmly established theoretical bases or generally agreed and tested methods of procedure as is the case in the physical and biological sciences. Psychology and still more sociology are, if not in their infancy, still very young, and taking them seriously does not demand taking the evaluation offered at any particular time by any particular practitioner or group of practitioners. But I assume that it is flying in the face of a great deal of evidence if one denies that psychology and sociology have formed and are forming many useful, and hitherto untried, tools for increasing our understanding of the realities which are to be found in the human condition.

Granted this, is it reasonable to hope that as the tools are refined and more widely used they will gradually erode the use of the notion of responsibility? I believe that we can see now, whatever be the state and true bearing of relevant psychological and sociological studies, that such a hope or, to put it more neutrally, expectation, would be profoundly unreasonable. Any such expectation on our part would not be reasonable in at least three senses of the term: the pragmatic, the logical and the evaluative. (These three senses are distinguished in order to make certain points. In practice they run into one another.)

It is pragmatically unreasonable to look for an erosion of the notion of human responsibility on the grounds that such an expectation would be implicitly claiming more than the facts warrant in at least two ways. Firstly, what factual grounds are there for supposing that psychology and sociology, however advanced and however combined, will be able to give a totally comprehensive account of the behaviour of either a human individual in his individuality or groups of human beings in the full complexity of their existences and interrelationships? In this connection there is the further point that psychology and sociology would not only be expected to produce a totally comprehensive account but also one generally and authoritatively agreed total account. The facts of the situation with regard to the 'state of the question' in psychology and sociology would scarcely seem to make it pragmatically reasonable (i.e. safe and desirable) to expect this. Much psychological talk is, when philosophically analysed, remarkably mythological (has anyone *really* observed a 'Kleinian' baby, still less a 'Freudian' id?), while much sociological talk has the presuppositions of the questionnaires and selection of evidence too strongly built into the conclusions to count as very strongly objective. And is there evidence that psychologists and sociologists agree among themselves to an extent which makes it reasonable to treat them as sole arbitrators on human questions? The notion of the object of psychological and sociological research as in some sense at least a potentially responsible being may well be a desirable safeguard against a misplaced claim to matter-of-fact omniscience about human beings.

Secondly, at this pragmatic level there is the question of the status of the expert in psychological and sociological understanding who finally decides or persuades others to the view that this man, or that class of men, or all men cannot be or should not be treated as responsible in any actual or potential sense. This is to put a particular sort of expert in a peculiar position of power *vis-à-vis* his or her fellow human beings. There would seem to be little in the commonly observed behaviour of ourselves and our fellows, however expert in whatever fields, to suggest that this type of power is desirable or safe. There would, therefore, seem to be a strong case for expecting to retain the notion of responsibility as a safeguard against arbitrary treatment of one class of human beings by another. That is to say that it is pragmatically unreasonable to expect a disappearance of the notion of responsibility because such a notion is 'a good thing' as a check on a misplaced claim to omniscience or a dangerous claim to omnipotence on the part of one class of human beings over the rest.

But it would seem to be not only desirable to retain the notion of responsibility, but also logically necessary—and we have already touched on the grounds for this in referring to the decision of the experts that some or all men are not responsible. We have here to consider the logic that is involved in the existence of judging and deciding subjects. To take a true decision that we are all wholly conditioned in all our deciding requires a subject whose decision, or judgement that this is so, logically transcends the conditioned decisions he is referring to. The decision that all men cannot be thought of as responsible must be taken responsibly and cannot in its taking include the taker. At another time, or indeed at the same time, the one who concludes that men do not have, or have the chance to have, responsibility, can be the object of observations to some other judging subject who may conclude that the first taker of the judgement is himself conditioned so that it is *not* a responsible

B

judgement. But we cannot eliminate one logically transcendent judgement made by a free and responsible subject. *How* this can be so may be logically very difficult to see. (Or impossible to see logically, as the determinists plausibly argue.) *That* this must be so is logically necessary. And no amount of the discovery of psychological and sociological facts or of the refining of theories can exempt the discoverers of the facts or the establishers of the theories from this logical necessity. Somewhere, someone needs to be free and responsible and to know something of what it is to be such, to be able to declare that there is no such thing as responsibility. Thus, whatever may be the difficulties of holding this notion of responsibility in face of the logical case for determinism, and the pragmatic case for finding more and more men more and more conditioned in a variety of ways, we are faced with the logical oddness of the decision that decisions are conditioned to the total exclusion of the notion of responsibility.

Just as the pragmatic unreasonableness of expecting the erosion of the notion of responsibility has features which lead on to a consideration of logical unreasonableness so a consideration of the latter leads on to an evaluative unreasonableness which ties back again with the pragmatic. Is it sensible of us as human beings to be ready to, or feel ourselves forced to, give up the notion of responsibility? If the facts compelled us to surrender this notion then whether we regretted the necessity or welcomed it, we would clearly have to give up the notion as sensible and rational beings, for 'facts' are, by definition, that which compels the acceptance of sane and rational persons. But under my 'pragmatic' heading I have suggested that there are no sufficient grounds for holding that the facts do or will compel us to surrender the notion of responsibility. Indeed it is sufficiently clear on reflection that to conclude that the facts produced by psychological and sociological investigation invite or compel us to give up the notion of responsibility is to take a decision which goes beyond the conclusive evidence of the facts themselves. The facts may point or tend to point in this direction, but the decision that it is reasonable to surrender the notion of responsibility has to be made with the help of other grounds.

I have further argued that the making of judgements, such as that men are not responsible, logically requires the existence and activity of a subject who is excluded from the scope of the judgement and who is free and responsible in making the judgement. I am not sure that I have set out the logical impossibility involved correctly, nor that if I have done so, or were to do so, everyone would whole-heartedly agree that it is a logical impossibility. Further the connection between what is logically impossible and what is actually the case is not entirely straightforward. I am not sure, therefore, that the logical unreasonableness of surrendering the notion of responsibility is a decisive reason for refusing to interpret psychological and sociological data in a way which destroys responsibility, although I suspect that it is. In any case it gives us further grounds for treating the question of what is reasonable in this sphere as a complex one involving several layers of interpretation and argument.

We are inquiring whether it is sensible to give up the notion of responsibility. Certain facts make this notion a difficult one, but there are pragmatic difficulties involved in giving it up. Further there is some case for holding that the notion is logically necessary. Thus we have reasonable grounds for resisting the tendency to dispense with the notion of responsibility if we see sufficiently compelling need to do so. This compelling need is not difficult to find. It is neither reasonable nor human to develop and encourage attitudes and judgements which have a tendency to encourage the treatment of men as less than human beings. But a man's responsibility for himself, for his actions and his relationships, is extremely important to, almost certainly essential to, his particular existence as himself, that is to say as a particular and unique person. And for other people to treat him as entirely without responsibility for himself is to refuse to grant him recognition as a full human being. Once a man has ceased to be regarded and treated as in any sense a responsible or potentially responsible individual he has simply become a case of some neurosis, some socially-conditioned disorder, some inherited pathological condition and the like. But this is to lose individuality and with it personality in the generality of classification. A man who is treated as nothing but a case of recognised classification has ceased to be treated as a man. And there is plenty of evidence available from more enlightened investigation of what went on, and still goes on, in some mental wards and prison blocks, that a man who is so treated becomes less able to be a man. There is also a growing body of evidence that men who present all the appearance and behaviour of being much less than responsible human beings, none the less, when treated as such, begin gradually to emerge as such.

This type of experience is an illustration of the way in which the pragmatic, the logical and the evaluative run together in our experience and treatment of human beings. This is precisely what Christians would expect, believing as they do that the whole material universe proceeds from the purpose of a God who is personal, and is capable of being moved towards the fulfilment of this personal purpose in the interrelationships of persons, derived from materiality, among themselves and with the personal God from whom everything depends and in whom everything is to be fulfilled. It is also what every humanist, atheist, theist or agnostic must hope. For the humanist is one who is moved to put his faith in those possibilities of matter, event and process which he perceives in the actualities and the potentialities of human beings. It would therefore seem quite clear that no human being who wishes to act and react as his shared humanness requires can possibly acquiesce in the decision that the concept of responsibility is to be dropped from our approach to human beings. He has no reasonable grounds for such a decision and no evidence can put him under sufficient rational or human compulsion to justify him in such a decision. He may be too cowardly or too trivial a person to be prepared to bother with responsibility or himself too damaged a personality to be able to cope with responsibility. But this is quite another matter, wherein the allegedly decisive pragmatic and logical reasons for dispensing with the whole notion are not exercises of rationality but of escapism, not of mature judgement but of immature weakness.

But while I have briefly touched upon a whole set of reasons at different levels which might seem to many to make it sufficiently clear that the notions of responsibility must not be and cannot be dispensed with, it remains clear on the other hand that there is much at the various levels which count against the notion of responsibility. The whole argument considered at the opening of this paper would never have arisen if this were not so. At the pragmatic level there is all the evidence which prompts psychologists, sociologists and criminologists to deny the usefulness of the concept; at the logical level there is all that is involved in the age-old free will–determinism debate; and at the evaluative level there is the great question raised by the need to talk of 'potentially responsible' and to defend the concept of responsibility.

In fact, in considering the question of responsibility we are brought up against the whole question of what it is to be human, what it is to be a person. But why should this be so? Might not the tie-up between being responsible and being a human person be simply the obsessive mistake of our guilt-ridden and activity-orientated Western civilisation? Here we are moving in on one of those fundamental questions which sometimes seem too general to be helpfully meaningful and which are always difficult to answer convincingly. The question is 'What are we to understand as being involved in being a man?' We have come to this question after starting with a current topic in social policy and research, viz. deviant behaviour and the question of responsibility. Our discussion of this topic has faced us with two sets of factors, one set of which must surely count as observables, the other set of which may perhaps count only as presuppositions.

The observables are those features of the human situation, and of our handling of and reflection upon human situations, which cause us to raise pragmatic and logical questions about the possibility or necessity of eliminating the notion of responsibility, or accepting determinism as a decisive last word about that situation. It is observably the case that the whole range of observables involved in the human situation cannot be fitted into any one frame of reference without a *choice* about which types of observables are to be decisively significant for the building of the interpretative frame of reference which is being commended. This last point draws our attention to the fact that our set of observable factors includes the observed fact that all interpretations of the human situation, including a claim for the elimination of the notion of responsibility or a plea for its retention, contain an evaluative element, i.e. judgements about the human situation are never, as far as can be seen, purely judgements about matters of fact, although they are not infrequently claimed as such. Thus it is pragmatically observable that there is 'more to' the human situation than can be accounted for or coped with by any one theory or any one discipline or line of study. The question is whether this 'more' is a pointer to a suggestive mystery or to a meaningless muddle.

This brings us to the other set of factors we have come across which may be a set of presuppositions only. They include what is involved in being concerned about the dangers or possibilities of the notion of 'responsibility' and what is implied by talk about treating criminals and others 'as persons'. All such talk involves the presupposition that there is something decisively important about 'being a person' and, when the notion of 'responsibility' is brought in, it also implies that 'being a person' is tied up with being, actually or potentially, an independent source of *my* actions (for which *I* can be held responsible). This implies the presupposition that it is important that 'I' should have the chance of being 'I'. I am not at all clear how this presupposition is to be justified or, alternatively, that it needs justification. At times it seems self-evident (if the argument about the unreasonableness of encouraging attitudes which encourage the treatment of men as less than human beings is accepted); but by no means all traditions of human thought accept this presupposition. It is not a presupposition which is universally acted upon (some human beings are more equal, to wit, more 'human' than others in the practice of most groups of human beings!). And there are grave practical grounds for doubting whether many, indeed most, or all human beings can have the chance of 'being I' (responsible human beings) in the manner desiderated (this is where the argument started). It seems therefore that we cannot avoid the question of faith. What do we put our trust in as giving us the stance from which we make our estimate of the human situation?

The argument being pressed here is that we should at least put our faith in the hint of the mystery of being a person which can be derived from the observables and the intuition of the value of being a person which is contained in the presuppositions of the type of arguing exemplified in what I have so far written. Further, the observable hint of mystery is to be tied up with the value intuited. It is the value perceptible in the possibility of being a person which strengthens the suggestion that the 'more to' the human situation (see p. 22) is a clue to a mystery rather than some epiphenomena or a muddle and, conversely, it is this observable 'more' which reasonably strengthens the claim that the value is to be perceived in and not merely read into the human situation.

But what is to be made of the fact that so much in the human situation seems to be contradictory of and opposed to the reality of responsibility? Here, I would suggest, we have to disentangle the notion of 'being responsible' in a present sense with a future reference related to being responsive, from that of 'being accountable' in a present sense with a past reference related to deserving praise or blame. In view of the past history of thought, both philosophical and theological, this is a tremendous piece of rethinking, the direction of which can be only briefly outlined here, but the line to be investigated would seem to be as follows.

The notion that in order to be responsible man must be able to be 'held responsible', that is, to be rightly praised or blamed, must be given up. There are two interconnected reasons for this. The first is that 'blameworthiness' and 'praiseworthiness' are not objective features of situations, actions or persons, but are simply reflections of subjective attitudes of praising and blaming. These (praise and blame) are attitudes arising in interpersonal relations and they reflect the states of mind of the persons involved and aspects of the relations between them. As indicators of these states of mind and relationships and as *raising* moral questions praising and blaming are, of course, of great significance. However, because of the subjective and personal nature of these activities, the mere *fact* of praising or blaming does not, in itself, indicate what is the moral significance of any particular circumstance or personal condition. Praising or blaming may reflect more of the pathology of the person indicating these attitudes than of the moral standing of that which or who is praised or blamed; e.g. the element of distaste for that of which we disapprove not only in criminals but, more importantly, in ourselves, is reflected in the belief that 'criminals' '*must*' be punished (referred to on p. 14). Thus 'accountability' in the sense of being judged worthy of praise or blame for past actions is not a reliable notion for assessing how responsible a man is.

Secondly, accountability for past actions turns out to be too complex a notion to be reliably assessed. Here the investigations of psychologists and criminologists backed up by the experience gained by any sensitive case worker or any person sensitively open to the past history of someone in trouble seem to make it sufficiently clear that the confident assignment of a particular action to a particular cause is just not justified. The more knowledge we have of the circumstances and conditions of human behaviour the less it seems possible to be assured that x is the responsible agent of his downfall, while y is the victim of circumstances. To understand everything may or may not lead to pardoning everything but more understanding certainly leads to less assurance about the validity of present assessments of past accountability.

The real question of responsibility seems to be, not that of accountability, but of how responsibility can be accepted now so that the area of responsibility can be enlarged. That is to say, how can a man be helped to accept himself for what he is and his situation for what it is and thus *accept* responsibility for being himself and so enlarge the area of his positive and personal response to his present circumstances and subsequent possibilities? In this sense the acceptance of responsibility is a necessary part of growth in being a person, a series of essential steps in becoming an independent centre of action rather than a determined focus of reaction. To be responsible is to be ready to learn how to come to terms with oneself and so to be set free to respond with more and more initiative to opportunities, circumstances and personal relationships. Responsibility is thus a present challenge and a future possibility which has to be evoked and assisted.

But if responsibility is so important to being human and personal what are we to make of the apparent fact that it is so threatened and threatening, so much more a potentiality rather than an actuality? Can any light be thrown on, or any perspective be given to, the apparently precarious and problematic nature of the human situation? Here I wish to juxtapose some reflections which cluster round the Christian tradition of the 'Fall'. For it is clear that the notion of the Fall has been one of the chief focusing points of the Christian tradition's reflection on the fact that there is a problem about being human or even that being human constitutes a problem. I make this juxtaposition because, being a Christian, I believe that the Christian tradition is a way of access to insights into the human situation which amounts to revelation of the truth and reality involved in that situation and of authentic and valid ways of understanding and responding to the situation.

The Biblical and Christian tradition makes its characteristic assessment of the problematic human situation by describing it as *sinful*. As will appear I believe this to be a better way of making this point than to say that the tradition sees the problem of the human situation as *caused by sin*. Thus the tradition is quite clear that every man is to be understood and, if he is to come to a healthy way of life, must understand himself, as a sinner. The primary meaning of this is that he is in a wrong relationship with God. The proper interpretation of the Biblical approach would seem to be that being in a wrong relationship with God is equivalent to being a sinner and vice versa. It is not the case that being a sinner causes a wrong relationship with God. The Bible does not appear to be concerned with causal categories but with defining situations in relationship to God.

None the less the question clearly arises as to why one is in a wrong relationship with God. This question can be interpreted in two forms. Firstly, of what does the wrong relationship consist? And secondly, what caused the existence of a state of 'being-in-a-wrong-relationship'? Now the most simple answer to the first form of the question would seem to be self-centredness as this is the antithesis to relatedness with God and with one's fellow men, wherein righteous, i.e. non-sinful, living, consists. So if one asks the second form of the question one is confronted with the question: what caused self-centredness? But we may wonder whether this is in fact a proper question. In a good many Christian theories it would seem that the suggestion is made that the Fall is the cause of the self-centredness. But this is not really an answer for in fact the Fall clearly stands for an assertion or expression of self-centredness. That is to say it would be equally true to say that self-centredness caused the Fall. We find therefore that what looks like an explanation is simply a symbolic description.

We may therefore inquire why we need to find an answer to the question about the cause of self-centredness or sinfulness. There appear to have been two main reasons for this. The first is that it seems necessary to exonerate God. Something is wrong with the human situation. God is good; therefore, we must ask what is the cause of the wrongness in the human situation and we must be able to answer it in a way which frees God from blame and therefore preserves his goodness. The second need for an answer to this question seems to lie in something to do with responsibility. There is a feeling that we must explain self-centredness in such a way that it does remain blameworthy and for it to do this responsibility must be preserved. If the situation does not have a cause which lies in a man's own power and choice, then he is not responsible for it. Hence a further reason for being interested in the cause of the Fall.

But is it reasonable to seek to exonerate God from responsibility for wrongness by finding a cause which explains wrongness? Would not an explanation of wrongness be a contradiction in terms? The problem would seem to be precisely that in the wrongness of the human situation we are faced with an inexplicable element, a surd. For example, if one were to construct an answer where it is shown that the Fall is a causal event which is necessary to the full maturity of human living, then we are showing how the Fall is good and therefore that it is not a fall in the sense of something which is causally explanatory of evil. (It is indeed likely that as we come to a better understanding of the dynamics of human development we shall see quite clearly that the 'wrongness' in the human situation is relateable to necessary stages in human development. This is one of the lines of investigation to be followed up. The only point being made here however is that talk about the Fall cannot do the job it is sometimes supposed to, viz. 'explain' evil.) I think it very likely that the Biblical approach is simply saying that evil is evil and cannot be turned into good by being subsumed into a wider system which gives it a good role.

The Biblical approach appears to be that we believe in God and that we know him to be good and that this knowledge and faith is maintained in the face of and despite evil which is none the less clearly recognised as evil. Because of this faith in God one is clear that evil does not have the last word about the nature of reality. (Clearly, with or without faith in God, evil does not have the *only* word upon the subject of reality, for there is also good.) Since this is the situation we have no need to 'exonerate' God, indeed we may well ask who are we to think that we should be in a position to do such a thing. The real question is, what does God do about evil? Unless there is evidence that he does do something about evil, clearly men of faith will eventually be convinced that he does not exist.

It would seem therefore that the first ground for being concerned with the cause of self-centredness does not stand. We therefore turn to the question about the cause of self-centredness raised in the interests of maintaining responsibility. Here we are obliged to observe the difficulties about assessing responsibility in relation to past actions and past cause discussed at length earlier. There would seem to be no point in asking 'Am I responsible for my self-centredness?' in the sense of hoping for an answer that I caused it over against anything else having caused it. The only possible question would seem to be, 'Am I, or can I be, responsible in my self-centredness?' Now the Bible would answer 'yes' to this question and that on two grounds. I am responsible because God addresses me as a responsible and human being, and secondly, I am responsible because there is a way forward into freedom to which I can assent or from which I may dissent. If God treats me as responsible by entering into a relationship with me to which I have something to contribute (compare, e.g. a covenant), then I have the opportunity of responding to this and I am responsible because I have the opportunity for this response. Further, when I am offered the opportunity through the grace of God, particularly as seen in Jesus Christ, to enter into freedom from the determination of my past history and my present character, then I am responsible in that I have the possibility of accepting or rejecting this freedom. But this means that responsibility emerges as I realise that I am in a situation in which I ought not to be and that I have the opportunity of being freed from this situation. Further, this will mean that I discover responsibility in the form of guilt, namely, awareness that I am in a situation in which I ought not to be, a situation which is sinful and, as it is my situation, I am in a guilty situation. Further, at the same time as I discover my guilt and my responsibility, I discover the possibility of my freedom. There is therefore a very close connection between guilt, responsibility and freedom. If I am to develop as a free person then I have to be able to accept responsibility for that in me which is both an essential part of me, feeds the development of myself as an 'I' and yet goes against the grain of my free and full development for it is a self-centredness which precludes the free relationship with others and with God, in and through whom alone I can grow as a person. The problem is, therefore, how I can receive the capacity to accept responsibility and so be enabled to nullify that in me for which I must be responsible (for it is part of me) and yet for which I am not responsible (accountable) in the sense that 'I' have developed this way and not produced this 'thing'.

All this would seem to mean firstly that we must not treat responsibility, guilt and freedom as if they were things which exist in their own right and which can be thought of as being caused by other things—like objects or situations. We are in fact using nouns to characterise aspects of relationships and situations. Secondly, we do not help our understanding of the situation by attempting to find a cause for human self-centredness. It is simply one of the facts of the situation. The relationship of this to the psychology of human development in which it becomes clear that self-centredness of a certain sort together with aggressiveness of a certain sort and development over against other people is necessary for growth needs careful investigation. Thirdly, human self-centredness when it reaches a self-conscious level, emerges as sin because it is manifested as a wrong relationship with God and a wrong relationship with man. Fourthly, we know this is so because of our experience. Man is 'at odds' with himself both in the sense of being an individual who is divided within himself and in the sense of being divided unsatisfactorily from his fellow men. We know this also from revelation which shows us man at odds with God. But fifthly, in the context of the Biblical and Christian revelation this knowledge is not an expression of pessimism but an assertion of good news. Evil is to be treated as evil and not just a homogeneous part of the totality of things. The discovery of the component parts of the situation is the discovery of the Fall, i.e. that the situation in which man finds himself has 'fallen' below the reality for which man is intended and to which he can attain. Therefore the doctrine of the Fall is not a pessimistic doctrine but one which implies the hope of wholeness and fulfilment. If one accepts the fallen and guilty nature of the situation then there is the possibility of liberation from this situation for a free development in relation to God and other men.

This possibility is centred upon forgiveness wherein the situation is acknowledged as wrong; responsibility for the situation is not denied, yet this does not involve condemnation and rejection but rather acceptance which sets free. As there is this possibility of being forgiven there is the possibility of accepting responsibility. This means that one may blame oneself for one's situation of self-centredness without the possibility of destruction which comes from condemnation, and once one can blame oneself one is becoming a free person who accepts responsibility for oneself and one is therefore on the way to being set free to live responsibly and freely. But we would seem to have to come to the conclusion that in the whole situation there is and can be no objective guilt to be removed nor any objective justice to be assuaged or appeased for such 'things' are not thing-like and therefore not objective. Only persons exist objectively and we are seeking with the help of experience and revelation to understand the situation in terms of personal relationships involving other people and God.

The picture we have, then, is that the important diagnosis of the wrongness of the human situation is that the personal relationships are wrong; but this is not a hopeless situation. Rather, it is to be understood as 'fallen', that is, it is not defined by its wrongness but the wrongness is to be understood in relation to a possible and an intended rightness. This rightness consists in a relationship with God and with others and permits full human freedom and development. The wrong situation can be put right by forgiveness; that is by acceptance of each person as in a wrong situation (in the wrong, and therefore guilty), but at the same time by treating him or her as an acceptable person. This forgiveness sets the condemned and accepted person free to face his or her real position, accept responsibility for it and therefore find the possibility of freedom both in it and beyond it. The basic source of power and forgiveness is found in God as he presents himself in Jesus Christ.

I would suggest that in this approach to the human situation the Christian understanding is wrestling with the same problem of the wrongness of the human situation as are philosophers, psychologists, criminologists, and so on when they are each in their own way confronting the difficulties of free will and responsibility in the face of actual human behaviour and its conditioning. The problems are being faced from different bases and therefore become looked at in different ways. The basis of the philosopher might broadly be described as logic in the general sense of the correct manner of thinking and using concepts. The basis of the sociologist, psychologist and criminologist is his assessment of the actual evidence of human behaviour in the various spheres which he particularly investigates, with this evidence arranged according to the theories which the relevant disciplines find currently most acceptable. The basis for the Christian approach lies in the believed revelation witnessed to in the Bible, given concrete expression in Jesus Christ and reflected on in the light of experience by the Christian tradition. The main creative point, however, is that it is and must be the same situation which is being investigated and reflected upon, and I would claim that it is indeed recognisably the same situation.

Hence if Christians are at all right in their belief that the revelation they are called to respond to is a true reflection of the character and purposes of the God who underlies and is concerned with all reality, it must be the case that a proper understanding of the human situation will grow as we learn how to combine the insights that arise from our various bases of approach when those approaches are themselves validly and authentically used. This would mean that we are required to view the whole situation in the light of the fullest possible scientific and empirical understanding, combined with a belief about the true context of the human mystery which includes an understanding of fallenness which comes from the development of the Christian understanding. There will be an interplay of interpretation here which will be difficult to maintain creatively, but which must be striven after. In the present situation where there is still a good deal of split between 'science' and 'religion' the self-appointed protagonists of each approach are liable to claim too much for themselves so that, for example, a new psychological theory is sometimes alleged to have finally driven all mystery out of the human situation while on the other hand claims are sometimes made on behalf of Christianity that certain scientific discoveries cannot be true and valid because they appear to contradict allegedly valid Christian insights. In fact both sides have to learn from one another. Scientific investigation has to expose the realistic and pragmatic structure of the human situation which is to be understood and lived in on the basis of the faith and hope pointed to by revelation. Any form of escapism from reasonably established facts must be contrary to the essential nature of the Christian understanding of revelation.

Finally one must add that it is in a faithful and hopeful approach to the human situation that Christians and non-Christians can combine in practice, in working for the development of that acceptance, responsibility and freedom, which would seem to be the essential shaping of humanness. For instance, there is a great need to have much more clarity about how much of the problem element, or element of wrongness in the situation and character of particular human beings and of human beings in societies and groups is to be rightly understood as due to what might be called sin and how much is due simply to the essential conditions for human growth. If I am to establish myself as a responsible being, for example, I would seem to be obliged to use a certain amount of self-assertiveness and indeed aggression; on the other hand assertiveness and aggressiveness clearly contribute greatly to the wrongness of many situations. Clearly therefore we need as clear an understanding as possible of the right and wrong uses of aggression. We need in fact to be able to distinguish the wrong relationship element in aggression and many other features of human living from the developing element. If we accept the whole thing as simply a development then we are at first being overoptimistic, for human development, as actually observed, clearly creates many problems. But if, when we have seen the impossibility of an optimistic view of development, we are unable to introduce any notion equivalent to that of fallenness we are then thrust into pessimism. Human development, in fact, seems more likely to have bad results than good. If, however, we may have grounds for the faith and hope expressed in the notion of fallenness, i.e. that we have to see the situation as a distortion of a necessary developing element by a wrong relationship element, then we may have grounds to steer realistically between an optimism which is destructive of a proper assessment of facts, and a pessimism which is destructive of a properly human approach. It is along lines such as these that I would hope for a fruitful dialogue on both theory and practice between all those concerned with a constructive approach to the human problems of responsibility, guilt and freedom.

2 HUMAN NATURE AND THE FALL

A Psychological View

In his autobiography Jung says that all his life has been devoted to trying to understand the nature of personality. This is the central mystery of human nature. Selfhood, self-identity, subjectivity, have to be seen from many aspects. We can only describe what we refer to by these terms, not explain the mystery. In the end we have to be content with experiencing what it is to be a human being and accept the mystery.

Systematic psychology is a comparatively new science but like all sciences it has many branches. Because it is so young and so fertile it has not achieved a commonly agreed set of concepts nor a terminology in which to express them, nor a unified structure as a science. It studies man externally by observing the many facets of his behaviour. It studies him internally by introspection. It traces his growth as an individual and compares him with the animals. It measures his intelligence and explores his dreams and fantasies. It examines him in sickness and in health. Out of the mass of material that has been accumulated, a picture of man is emerging which is clear in its main features, and though we know it is far from the whole truth and may be distorted by overemphasis in this or that direction, it is nevertheless sufficiently established to compel us to re-examine conclusions about man which were formulated without the information which psychology in all its branches has brought to us.

I propose to consider a few of the main points which have emerged and their significance for religious thought, particularly what light they throw on the concept of the Fall of Man.

c

The Unity of Body and Mind

The first concerns the relationship of body and mind. This is an intractable problem in the present state of our knowledge, but it is an important one because of a tendency in some quarters to seek a full explanation of mental changes in terms of chemical or electrical processes in the body, particularly in the glands or the central nervous system.

The separation of matter and mind into two incommensurable orders was first systematically formulated by Descartes. It cleared the way for remarkable advances in the physical sciences, but has created apparently insoluble problems for the biological and psychological ones. The separation makes mental phenomena to be so different in kind from bodily phenomena that they cannot be described in terms appropriate to the latter. Yet the evidence seems to show that there is some bodily process correlated with every mental one. Every mind is embodied and would therefore appear to derive its existence and functioning from the body. It is by no means so evident that there is a mental correlate to every bodily activity, but some of the phenomena from nervous disorders and behaviour under hypnotism justify our maintaining it as a working hypothesis.

We seem to have to choose between three theories of the relationship between mind and body. The first of these is known as epiphenomenalism, because it treats the mind as a by-product of the functioning of the body. Action is only in one direction, from the body to the mind, and apparent causal connections between mental events are really due to the connections between the underlying bodily processes. The mind cannot act upon the body. If this theory is correct we must seek the ground of mental and spiritual progress solely in the adequate functioning of the body. It seems so contrary to ordinary experience that we should not need to take it seriously were it not that the results of research in bio-chemistry and biophysics are frequently presented as though they gave a complete explanation of mental functioning.

The second theory postulates that mind and body are two series of events which run parallel to each other. They cannot interact because they are different in kind, incommensurable. The parallelism has to be accepted as a fact, but possibly what we observe as two series with apparent interconnections may be the result of looking at the same things in two different ways, or from two different aspects. What from an interior aspect we see as mental may appear as bodily when viewed exteriorly. To unify the two series in this way would demand a renunciation of the Cartesian division, but so far the new category of thinking has not emerged.

The most acceptable theory is that of interactionism, which declares that the facts of experience which point to the interaction of mind and body cannot be brushed aside in the interests of doctrinaire assumptions. Clearly experience (and experiment) indicates that an activity of the whole person sometimes originates in the body, sometimes in the mind. Mind can influence body and body mind, so there must be a dynamic interrelationship, even if we are unable to formulate it in suitable terms. Hence in our understanding of man we must see him as mind and body, never simply as mind or as body. When his body dies, his mind disappears from the space-time order or our experience here on earth. Similarly his body changes its character and ceases to function as a human body, becoming only an aggregate of parts, which soon disperse.

We may perhaps recollect in this connection that the Christian Creed has always asserted that there cannot be a human life, in this or any other conceivable mode of existence, which is not an embodied life. It is no part of Christian belief to maintain what has been called 'the ghost-in-the-machine' idea of man. He is a psychosomatic unity in the sense that he is part of this world order by virtue both of his body and his mind. In throwing out the 'ghost' we must be careful not to be left with a machine on our hands, and nothing more.

Man and Evolution

If we accept the unity of body and mind in man we are compelled to see him, both biologically and psychologically, in the perspective of natural evolution. Man belongs to the order of animals, but he has so far outstripped the others in the range and complexity of his mental development that theologically he has been contrasted with them, and it is only in modern times that his true affinity with them has been recognised and adequate consideration of his animal inheritance becomes possible. Nevertheless we should not fall into the opposite error of underestimating the significance of man's advance from the other animals. Man is aware of himself as a person, able to observe his own mental processes and reflect on them; that is, he has self-consciousness, which so far as we can see, the other animals have not. And man's power of communicating with his fellows and of storing information in books, pictures, and so on, is infinitely beyond the capacity of the animals. Though it is not so obvious, there has been a similar advance in his bodily capacity, not so much in the grosser forms of muscular effort but in the development of his brain, and particularly of its highest levels, giving him much more complex modes of interconnection and control in the brain and the capacity to learn from experience. In other words, man's body is not just an animal body; it is a human body adapted to and carrying the mental powers he possesses. Certainly we cannot neglect man's resemblance to the lower animals, but the differences are even more important. We must not be misled by the coarser features of structure or function into assuming that what seems bodily determined in man will have the same form as it has in the lower animals. Man is always specifically man, never 'merely animal'.

It is in relation to the instincts—sex, aggression, self-preservation, etc.—that it is most important to bear this caution in mind. They are commonly thought of as the animal part of man. But instincts in man, though derived like everything else in his native endowment from his animal forebears, have evolved to their special human form. In the animals, instincts tend to follow a fixed pattern characteristic of each species; and the capacity for variation is very limited. The patterns are innately fixed so that there is little scope or need for learning by experience.

In man, on the other hand, only the very broad lines of instinctive behaviour are determined innately, and seemingly end-less variation is possible to him through the ability to learn by experience. The driving power inherent in his instincts becomes diverted from the simple animal ends to supply the motivation of the whole range of human conduct. Man's constitution has been modified in evolution to enable this to happen, otherwise he would not be man. If we ascribe 'animal instincts' to man, in the sense of impulses which push him into behaviour identical with that of animals and without the mental and spiritual concomitants proper to man, we are refusing to face the fact of his evolution. His instincts are human, not merely animal.

It is a fallacy to suppose that there is a 'natural' man who would instinctively behave like the animals were it not for the conditioning of society and the restraints it imposes on him, and that we can ob-serve this in primitive, undeveloped forms of society. The most primitive man we know is as much conditioned as the most civilised, perhaps more so. It is man's nature to require education. Without it he would be helpless. He becomes what his environment stimu-lates and conditions him to become. This is his nature. It is as 'natural' for him to eat food cooked as to eat it raw, as 'natural' for him to enjoy poetry as copulation. His nature is such that he develops such tastes in the course of his growth. He must at all times be thought of as human. Only on this condition is it safe to compare him with the animals.

We cannot then divide man into 'lower' and 'higher' parts of himself, one being the 'natural' and the other the 'spiritual'. That man may be divided is a fact of observation, but the division is not along these lines. We must not seek the explanation of the Fall of Man in the persistence in him of an animal inheritance which wars against his spiritual self.

The Social Matrix

Man learns by experience and is conditioned by the environment in which he grows, but he is not simply a product of the environment. He is a centre of active energy reaching out to the world around him,

seeking expression of his innate, instinctive drives. What he becomes is always the resultant of the interaction between himself
and his environment.

In the first two years of his life his mother is almost the whole of
his effective environment since his major and most frequent contacts with the world are through her. He is not aware in this period
of his own separate individuality; he has not reached the stage of
self-consciousness, of awareness of himself as a separate person.
Nor can he know that his mother is a person independent of him.
He is aware only of what he experiences, the sensations and the
pleasures and pains accompanying them. It is only when he attains
self-consciousness, somewhere about the age of two, that he is able
to understand that he is one among a group of persons and see
them and the world over against himself. The borders of demarca-
tion are only gradually defined as he grows and he may never
completely separate self from not-self. Consciousness of selfhood
does not come automatically. The adult sees the baby as an individual set in his environment, but the baby has to grow into this
knowledge.

His personality emerges out of the matrix of his experiences in
a social setting. Society comes before the individual. This is
part of the humanness of man; it does not mean that society should
have precedence in value over the individual. It means that the
individual cannot be abstracted from society without destroying
an essential part of his humanity. He is in a real sense an individua-
tion of the society in which he has grown up. His personality is built
up out of the experiences he has had in reaction to the world of
persons and things of which he is a part. In his first two years before
he has come to self-consciousness he has undergone a wealth of
experience which goes far to shaping the pattern of his personality.
This point has been made by many writers, but seldom with the
clarity and force that John Macmurray gives it in his Gifford
Lectures, *Persons in Relation*.

Two main lines of study, complementary and not mutually
exclusive, open up from this. We may study society and the inter-
relations of the individuals who compose it, or we may study the

ideas, feelings and motives of the individuals. I propose to confine myself to the development of the individual, always bearing in mind, of course, that he exists only in the context of society. In thus limiting myself I am well aware of the importance and value that must be attached to contributions on the other aspect, such as those of Argyle and Eysenck. But these only emphasise the need to supplement them with a study of the inner functioning of the mind.

Growth

The individual cannot be understood in his wholeness unless we adopt the developmental point of view and take into account the changes in the structure and functioning of his mind which take shape as he grows. These are particularly important in the early years, up to about six. The young child differs from the adult not only in the extent of his knowledge but also in the way he thinks and feels. For instance, he does not possess a moral sense or conscience like that of an adult. I shall return to this later. At this point I want to stress that his growth brings more than the accumulation of experiences. The effect of those experiences in early childhood is to bring about alterations in the structure and functioning of his mind.

This structure is complex. It is the resultant of the innate drives on the mental level, meeting the pressures which come to him from the world outside him, personal and non-personal, direct and indirect. He is not a *tabula rasa* on which the world imprints its own exact image. He is a reacting organism, selecting, adapting, assimilating from the world according to his inner needs. Some of his experiences of the world are encouraging, some discouraging. He experiences love, pleasure, hope, fear, anxiety, frustration, deprivation, rage, security and insecurity, guilt and forgiveness, and these have to be built into his total self.

This is not the place in which to trace the various stages in the formation of the mind as we know it in the adult. In the rest of this chapter I shall simply take three aspects of the mind for fuller consideration: the unconscious, the process of sublimation, and the function of morality as revealed in the ego-ideal and super-ego. From the study of these we can get some understanding of the divisions in the mind and how a man can find himself at odds with himself and with God. Terminology becomes a difficulty in discussing them. To speak of structure is likely to invoke spatial images, as though the mind were divided into parts, whereas what is involved is the dynamic interrelation of various processes or functions of the mind. The model is dynamic, not static.

The Unconscious

The most important discovery in modern psychology about the nature of man is that part of the mind is unconscious. In every one of us there is a section of our mental activity which is cut off from consciousness. The elements in it, images, fantasies, ideas, wishes, feelings, are active and powerful and are constantly striving to enter consciousness and get expression in behaviour. When we examine why this part of the mind is unconscious, beyond the reach of our ordinary efforts to get at it, we find that there is another part of the mind which is repressing it, that is, keeping it from emerging into consciousness by exerting pressure against it, and that this repression is itself unconscious. There are thus two parts at least of the unconscious, one repressing, the other repressed.

When we give an account of ourselves, our ideas and feelings, we can only do so in terms of what is in consciousness or can be called readily into consciousness. We only know ourselves in part. Since we are not aware of what is in the unconscious part of our mind we are apt to act as if it did not exist. But to ignore it is not to destroy it. The energy constantly being generated there must find an outlet. If the repressing force blocks all modes of expression, there comes a point when the whole system of force and counter-force must collapse, resulting in a mental breakdown. Usually the conflict does not continue to this point. A safety valve is found in compromise formations, through which the repressed urges can get expression and relief of tension, yet which are sufficiently far from the original form of the repressed matter to satisfy the censoring scrutiny of the repressing forces. Such compromise formations enter into behaviour in an infinite variety of ways—character traits, dreams, neurotic symptoms, anxieties, phobias, guilt feelings, obsessions, compulsive acts and so on. The conscious ego tries to assimilate them by rationalising them; that is, by explaining them in terms acceptable to the conscious system, as if they belonged only to that. The rationalisation is rarely completely successful, because echoes of the unconscious conflict rise uneasily to consciousness in the form of guilt feelings, anxieties, or anger, when the particular form of behaviour is questioned. Whether or not the guilt feeling is strong, we are all prone to a sense of insufficiency, of failure, or unworthiness. We are afraid that we are not lovable and our capacity to give our love freely is diminished. We feel cut off from our fellows, rejected by them, and we question our right to exist. This is more than a sense of sin, though it may take that form. It is a sense of not-being. It may lead us to long for God, but we cannot accept a God who loves us, because that would be to affirm that we are lovable, which we dare not do.

The existence of the unconscious is a limitation on the freedom of the conscious ego, and the more active the unconscious pressures, that is, the greater the extent of the repressions, the severer the restriction. The conscious ego is the executive part of the total personality, its representative to the world, but since it feels what is in the unconscious to be disruptive to its own control it has to fight against it. The compromise formations reached are not chosen by the ego; they are forced on it, and the ego maintains an illusion of freedom by constructing rationalisations to explain and appear to assimilate the alien elements. The unconscious puts us in bondage to ourselves.

By means of special techniques it is possible to bring to light some of the contents of the unconscious. To the conscious mind they may appear horrifying, for they include incest, parricide, perversions, obscenities, cruelty, and lust on an unbridled scale. The existence of such motives, powerful as they are, is not to be explained by the general depravity of man. They derive from the premora

years of infancy when the child was naturally and innocently completely egoistic and had no standards by which to regulate his
desires. As he acquires standards such desires are thrust down into
the unconscious, rejected by the controlling part of the total self.
In the course of normal development they lose their strength and
cease to be troublesome, but if, as happens in some degree almost
universally, there are failures in development, the repressed desires
may remain strong and influence thought and conduct in the ways
indicated above.

One mode of defence by the ego against them is to project the
inner conflict outwards. Two forms of this projection are of special
interest in religion. In one of these, the 'evil' temptations are seen
as coming from an outside source—the world or the devil—threatening the purity of the self. The self by projection has got rid of its
sense of uncleanness, but has to resist the evil which assaults it. In
the other form, closely allied, the self takes up attitudes of moral
indignation against all signs in the outside world of those 'evils'
which are strong in the unconscious and strives to have them
punished and suppressed by every means possible. Morality of this
sort is not true morality. It is only the symptom of mental dis-
harmony.

Neither repression nor externalisation of repression by projection
is a cure for the impoverishment of the self which is the result of
such a state. The techniques of cure differ, but it always involves
acceptance of the whole self, repressed and repressing, and acceptance of reality. A condition of achieving this acceptance is experience
of an atmosphere of acceptance and love, dispassionate love and
concern, which is supplied by a psychotherapist, a counsellor, or a
therapeutic group. Once the sufferer is enabled to face himself as
he is in his totality and accepts as his what he has been trying to
reject, he experiences what is really forgiveness and the power
disappears from the hitherto repressed desires. They are eliminated
if there is no place for them in the new self which results. I have
known people who have gone through this process of healing speak
of it as being 'born again'.

Sublimation by Diversion

Something needs to be said about sublimation, since it is frequently advocated as a method of dealing with repressed forces. There is considerable confusion about the proper meaning of the term. It is frequently used to describe the process by which urges which are inhibited by reason of circumstances, or for social or moral reasons, are diverted to socially acceptable outlets. For instance, a woman who cannot have children of her own without disapproval, because she is unmarried, may find satisfaction for a strong maternal instinct in nursing or teaching; or a child showing an insatiable curiosity may be turned to the study of history or science. In this way subsequent emotional conflicts may be avoided. So sublimation in this form is regarded as an essential part of educational aims and can be to some extent planned.

It is not a great step to apply the term to the diversion of repressed urges to socially approved forms. An example of this would be if a man with a strong unconscious urge to cruelty became a surgeon. Instead of having to fight down his unconscious impulse he could then indulge it, but to an end which brought him praise instead of condemnation. But when the impulse is unconscious such sublimation must take place spontaneously. The nature of the repressed urge is hidden, so a suitable diversion cannot be consciously planned. It is futile to advise a neurotic to sublimate his repressions.

Sublimations, however, occur very frequently. I spoke above of the infinite variety of compromise formations which may issue from unconscious conflicts to give repressed desires the expression they must have. Some of these are themselves incapacitating to a greater or lesser extent, neurotic illnesses, for example. But many take the form of socially useful activities, such as that of the surgeon satisfying his cruelty in his valuable work, or the clergyman giving vent to his hidden exhibitionism in the pulpit or at the altar.

Religion is a field which attracts such sublimations, partly because its roots are so deep in the self, partly because its central ideas, God, heaven, judgement, expiation, forgiveness, are so closely allied to infantile conceptions of the parents, and partly because religion has come to be associated with a strong moral condemnation of evil, with an implied demand for punishment. Some people turn to religion because they are heavily repressed and they find in it satisfaction of their repressions, protection against them, and the sense that they have chosen the most approved way of life, thereby compensating for their deep insecurity. I am not here referring only to the moralistic and self-righteous, but to numbers of people who are living devoted lives of sacrifice and service to their fellow men. Of course such a form of compromise with their unconscious is not to be condemned. If there is to be a compromise and not a cure it is very much to the good for them and for society that it should take a form which is socially valuable. Lack of money, time, and of people able to undertake it puts most treatment out of the question. I should add that a cure would not be likely to take away their religion. It would be more likely to deepen and confirm it.

The danger, however, in such a sublimation is that the unconscious element may get the upper hand and manifest itself more and more strongly in conduct, overemphasising self-righteousness and moralism. Or some upset may occur which causes a reversion to the unsublimated or a less desirable form, as with a man of my acquaintance who, when his young wife died suddenly, turned from a devout believer into an atheist overnight. Dominance by the unconscious leads easily to fanaticism, excessive cruelty, insatiable demands for punishment of oneself or of offenders against law and morals. In extreme cases it leads to religious mania. Where religion is a replacement for unresolved repressions, therefore, there is always an element of precariousness in it and it should not be mistaken for fully healthy religion.

True Sublimation

What we have been considering proves to be a diversion or displacement of instinctive urges from their original ends and forms to secondary ones, whether consciously or unconsciously. It would be better to think of this displacement as substitute satisfaction and reserve the term sublimation to denote another process in which

there is a transformation of energy from the instincts into cultural
and spiritual activities which are permanent and exist in their own
right. They develop out of the primitive instinctive urges, but as
part of normal growth, not as substitutes. The process is a complex
one. It has been most closely studied in relation to the development
of the 'sexual' instincts. (I use the term here in the technical psycho-
analytic sense, as I go on to explain.) Since these are in any case the
chief sources of energy for cultural and spiritual activities we may
look there to see how religion grows out of the primitive urges. By
calling them primitive urges I do not imply the 'merely animal' view
of man's sexual urges, for instincts in man have evolved, as I pointed
out above, beyond the forms to be found in the lower animals. But
the sensual and bodily urges form a kind of central core to the
sex instincts. Perhaps we may liken them to the trunk of a tree
which sends out many branches and whose life depends not
merely on its root system in the earth but also on the functioning
of its leaves in the light and air. The healthy functioning of the
sex instincts in man requires not only the activity of the biological roots but also the transforming activity of the higher levels of
growth.

This becomes more obvious if we look at two aspects of the
working of sex in man. The first is related to his self-consciousness.
We may suppose that the animals, under the impulses of their
sexual instincts, live in the immediate present and do not construct
imaginative pictures of the future, whereas man's consciousness
enables him to do so. He can anticipate the future more or less
correctly. He is aware of pleasures and pains, the tensions and longings, the hopes and frustrations, which accompany falling in love
and the desire to mate with the partner chosen. He is not simply
under the pressure of bodily needs. His body cannot function without stirring his mind into action. It may be that the physiological
processes generate the pressures which are the beginning of sexual
activity, but they are transmuted into mental forms in which the
mind looks ahead to anticipate the future. This opens up the possibility of choice between different lines of action. Because of the
complex nature of man and human society, the fulfilment of the

sexual urges involves a wide range of activities and of feelings and any of these may become the focal point of the aims which develop out of the urges. A man may focus his desire on the pleasure he gets from his body in coition and see little else in sex but that; or, on the other hand, he may find in it, and express through it, deep spiritual values which turn around his valuation of his partner. In the first case sexual satisfaction is little removed from the bodily, in the second it becomes of a sacramental nature. The union of bodies expresses and deepens the union of personalities. In between lie all manner of variations. The point I am making is that in man the mental and spiritual concomitants of sex are essential to its completeness.

The second aspect of sex which we should consider is the developmental one. In this we at once run up against the difficulty of terminology. The word sex is by long usage associated with the mating instinct we see functioning in adults. It is extended to apply also to subsidiary activities and derivative impulses, such as perversions, which are obviously related to the excitation of the genital organs or which intensify the desire to seek a sexual partner. But the adult sexual instinct is itself only one derivative of a more general group of instincts which are active in the child from birth and which at first do not function in relation to the genitals. The lines of development from these early instinctive forms to the adult form of mating can be clearly traced, so the early forms also deserve to be called sexual. Their connection with the adult form is very plain by the fourth year of life. In spite of being non-genital in the earlier years, the impulses and their attached feelings are no less intense.

The adult activity of sex, coming to its fullness after puberty, is merely one strand in the development through which these instincts pass. Not all the energies of the infantile forms flow into it. Much is diverted into other activities which, if we narrow the term 'sex' to the adult mating instinct, are non-sexual. This occurs because various inhibitions, coming from both internal and external sources, turn the instincts away from their objects and ends and compel them to other modes of action. They become in large part 'desexualised' and diverted to more general cultural forms. "Civilisation," said Freud, "is built upon the repression of sex." He was referring here to the infantile forms of sex, not the adult. But it is the channels through which the primitive energies flow which are changed, not their source. The energies supporting man's general cultural life come from the same source as his straightforward sexual desires. The wide diversion from directly sexual activities is possible first, because of the flexibility of instincts in man as compared with the animals, and, second, because of the pressures which the structure of the family, and society in general, brings to bear upon the infant.

These two great branches stemming from the primary sexual sources may come into conflict with each other. A man's sexual impulses may be contrary to his religious, social, moral or cultural values, and he has to try to find some compromise between them. He is involved in inner conflict. The degree of intensity of the conflict depends upon what has happened in the particular individual in his growth from birth onwards. One side or the other may have been over- or underdeveloped by the accident of circumstances, but the problem of reconciling the two remains for all people. To exalt the cultural over the sexual is a false solution. Of course it may be proper for certain individuals to renounce sex in favour of some ideal, but renounce should not be understood, particularly for them, as denounce. They have given up something of worth in itself. Healthy personality, full spiritual development, needs the harmonisation of the two strands in an all-inclusive ideal. Sex is not just a bodily appetite; it is a mental and spiritual matter, equal with the de-sexualised cultural expressions of the same basic energies. On the other hand, religion, education, morality, art and culture generally are not a second best, a mere substitute for something we are denied by the taboos of society. They are permanent ends essential to human development.

It is in this sense that 'sublimation' should be used. If there is deep and intense unconscious conflict within the personality we may get an apparent sublimation in these activities; but the fact that such false sublimations are frequent ought not to blind us, as it did Freud in *The Future of an Illusion*, to the part all the aspects of culture play in the full development of man as man. They are as essential to his well-being as is sex.

Aggression

I have used the example of the sexual instincts to show how the primitive urges have to be transformed and developed to make the characteristic human personality. In a similar way the instinct of aggression, which is also very powerful, has to undergo transformation if it is to play its full part in the making of a human being. There is this difference, however, that except in direct combat in war there is very little opportunity for the unrestricted exercise of the bodily forms of attack to which the instinct urges, as there is in sexual union for that instinct. Perhaps boxing and blood sports come nearest to it, but for the most part aggression is only allowed a partially free expression, as in other competitive sports and non-sporting contests, in commerce, and in politics, national and international.

Aggression is greatly subject to repression and therefore unconsciously influences behaviour to a very marked degree. One particular form of this, its entry into morality, is of special interest to us, and I shall have more to say about that presently. But it is probably true to say, as Freud indicated in *Civilisation and its Discontents*, that unresolved aggression is the greatest threat which culture and civilisation face in the world today. We will continue to live precariously until we learn how to absorb and transform our aggressiveness.

As with sex there are many pseudo-sublimations of repressed aggression. We take up the fight against war and crime, oppression and exploitation, against disease, poverty, squalor and ignorance, against all manner of social evils. We express our aggressiveness by word or pen in attacking that or those which we dislike, and we vent our anger and our hatred in righteous crusades. Of course our adoption of such causes may be the result of a real transformation of the primitive instinct to fight, especially when there is a clear positive ideal for which we are fighting, but in my belief it is the fighting which gives satisfaction in most instances rather than the ideal for which we fight.

The basic problem is to reconcile love and aggression in the human personality and in the relations of individuals and groups with each other. The primitive aim of aggression is to destroy, whereas love seeks to serve and to build up. There is no reconciliation in one of the two being completely suppressed, for this will only drive the struggle into the unconscious and the results may be disastrous. The reconciliation is only achieved when aggression is transformed and becomes the servant of the developed love impulses. Transformed aggression will show itself in tenacity of purpose, in a heightened sense of individuality, and in vigorous striving to further the welfare of others. It is a vital element in the mature personality. To achieve this desirable state will not be an easy task. The structure of our society and the ideals of conduct which are currently dominant are such as to encourage aggression untransformed or at best barely disguised. We do not fully realise the true nature and the inward character of the danger in which civilisation stands. We are content with too low a view of what a man is or could be.

The Fall or the Rise of Man

This low view of the nature of man has been enshrined in the doctrine of the Fall of Man and Original Sin.

In theology the Fall of Man has been treated as in some sense an actual event. The essence of the argument is that man was created innocent of sin, completely obedient to God, with an unbroken communion with him. Something happened to break this communion. The story of Adam and Eve and man's first sin is intended to explain the alienation from God, for we all are children of Adam and inherit the consequences of that sin. We may reject the story as history, but we cannot thus dismiss the facts which it seeks to explain: man's awareness of a constant bias towards wrongdoing in his behaviour and his own inability to cope with that bias. We can all understand and sympathise with St. Paul's agonised cry, "The evil that I would not, that I practise." It is not merely that we know

D

we have sinned; we are aware, when we are honest with ourselves, that we cannot help doing so.

In the face of this fact theology seems confronted with the choice of believing, on the one hand, that God deliberately created us as sinners, rebelling against him and choosing (if, indeed, we have any choice) that which must not only offend him but also destroy ourselves, and, on the other, of postulating some event, connoted by the Fall, in the beginning of time, or beyond time, by which man's original nature has been changed and he has become, as it were, infected by sin, from which he can only be cleansed by the grace of God.

I do not propose to speak of the difficulties inherent in this conception. I shall only speak about the light that psychology can throw on the problem. Psychology as such must confine itself to the description of man's behaviour and its explanation in terms of the perceptions, imaginations, ideas, emotions, motives, sentiments, and so on, which constitute his mind. It is true that most of these mental processes refer to a reality beyond the mind, a real world of things and people where the acting, thinking self has a place, a world which acts upon him and on which he acts and re-acts. The psychologist finds a very important distinction between pure fantasy and reality-orientated thinking. The dominance of the latter over the former is a condition of mental and spiritual health. Nevertheless, the hysterical pain in the abdomen is just as much a fact as the pain from appendicitis, and John Smith's claustrophobia is a state of real fear, though no danger threatens him. Hence the psychologist gets into some difficulty in trying to define what he means by reality. He uses the term 'psychological reality' as an escape. That John Smith has a repressed, and therefore unconscious, wish to murder his father is a fact of the same order that Tom Jones has murdered his father. But in John Smith's case the onlooker sees that he has not carried into action the impulse he unconsciously holds. To the onlooker, if he is aware of John Smith's impulse, it remains a wish. But that part of John Smith's mind, his unconscious, in which he has buried the impulse, has no power of discriminating between what is real and what is merely wish in the way that the onlooker does, or even John Smith's conscious mind does. To his unconscious mind, wishing to murder his father is the equivalent of what murdering his father would be to his conscious mind. This is what the psychologist means when he says that an unconscious wish has 'psychological reality'.

When it is the question of the nature of 'objective reality', that is, the world over against psychological reality, the psychologist suffers from the same difficulties as anybody else in trying to say what it is. He has, for the sake of intercommunication, to accept generally agreed ideas about it, merely correcting such conceptions as he is able to do because of the knowledge gained through his particular studies. The doctrine of the Fall of Man and the facts which appear to support it come within this category.

The two major facts which underlie the doctrine, the sense of having sinned, with its concomitant feeling of guilt, and the sense of unworthiness, are natural functions of the human mind, and they are normal factors in healthy growth, except where they are over- or underdeveloped. In other words, their presence in man is not the sign that something has gone wrong in his development as man. They are part of his growth to the attainment of full human personality. The dilemma in which the theologian thought he was placed is a false one, springing certainly from an inadequate understanding of the human mind and possibly also from a misconception of how God carries out his purposes. The latter point, of course, falls outside the scope of the psychologist.

Let me take first the sense of having sinned. By this I do not only mean conscious recognition of the actual sin we have committed. I mean that it is part of a man's moral nature to feel that he has sinned, whether or not he has done so in actual fact. But this sense of being a sinner is not given at birth, not something which he inherits; it is something which he acquires as he grows. Further, it is not a failure of growth; it is essential to his coming to full humanity. Without it he could not be a moral being.

The development of conscience by the individual is a very complex process. In examining its working there are two aspects to consider: the content of conscience, that is, the actual principles

accepted as the moral code to be followed; and the structure of the
mind which gives to an individual the sense of obligation which
characterises moral 'oughtness'. By means of the latter the individual directs and passes judgement on his own conduct, and he
can only be a moral being to the extent that he is able to do so.
Anyone who for some reason has a 'diminished sense of responsibility' is thereby the less a moral person. It is this moral sense which
constitutes the greater problem. The acquisition of particular moral
standards is easier to follow.

The infant begins its life with only the potentials of a mind, that
is, certain innate needs or drives for satisfaction: the faculty of
consciousness (not self-consciousness) and the senses which supply
the materials for consciousness to work on, the power of using
imagery, and memory as a storehouse, with recall as the way of
drawing on it. But he has no words—these have to be acquired—and
without words generalisations are impossible. This means that the
very shape and texture of his mind and personality, and the tools
his mind uses—images, emotional reactions, words and ideas later
—grow out of his experiences as a dynamic, sentient being in the
world he has entered.

I have spoken earlier of how the infant comes to consciousness
of self at about the age of two or a little earlier. He then knows that
he and his mother are separate persons. Before that, of course, he
was able to recognise his mother, because she was the constantly
recurring pattern of all his most intense experiences of pleasure and
pain. She was his world and he inevitably related all experiences,
good and bad, to her. He loved her and needed to feel her love flow-
ing out to him at all times. Without it not only would life be unbear-
able, he would find it hard to accept his own reality as a person.
It is not enough to say that he is dependent on her; that is far too
colourless a description. It is not even enough to say that he loves
her. His whole being reaches out to her, and he thinks that she re-
gards him in the same way. He identifies himself with her, not
consciously by imitation but unconsciously trying to live in her,
become what she is and do what she wants. The greatest calamity
of his life is to lose her love, and the fear of this is the strongest

sanction governing his conduct if he is led into anything which displeases her. Her approval and disapproval are the dominant factors controlling him.

Before he can be called a moral being, these dependent sanctions of approval and disapproval have to be internalised. This takes place by means of the struggle with the Oedipus complex which is the next main stage of his development. Once he has separated himself from his mother he goes on rapidly to sort out other people who previously had formed a penumbra around the central pattern he has constructed out of his experiences of her. Of these his father is the most significant. He becomes the great ideal of what the boy wants to be. At the same time he is a dreaded rival for possession of the mother and her love. (I do not need to elaborate since this aspect of the Oedipus complex is well known.) Fear of the father as well as love and admiration for him have been added as sanctions for the boy's conduct, alongside those derived from his love for his mother.

The conflict intensifies within the boy and he seems to be caught in an insoluble dilemma—to keep his mother, who is the meaning of life and love for him, and be destroyed by his omnipotent rival for doing so, or to obey what he imagines his father demands and give up his mother and the love and satisfactions which attach to her. The way out is opened up because of his identification with his father. He internalises the image he has formed of him with the unquestioned power and authority belonging to it. This he does by intensifying his identification, becoming his father, as it were, and giving himself the orders which he imagines come from him. He thus gains the strength to renounce his attachment to his mother, his claim for sole possession of her. The introjected image of his father becomes a permanent part of his mental structure, a super-ego, which henceforth is the seat of authority in him. He is now giving orders to himself. The internal authority has replaced the external sanctions as the final court of appeal about conduct. He has become a moral person, a complete human being, however much he still has to learn about particular standards to be applied by his new conscience.

I have spoken here in terms of the boy's development. The girl grows along a different line, not simply by reversal of masculine and feminine, with important consequences to the structure and functioning of her personality. It is not possible to go into all the complexities here, but the chief factors to note are the following. First, the mother is the first love object of the girl as of the boy and therefore when the father is recognised as a separate person the girl also sees him as a rival. Second, because of our innate predisposition towards heterosexuality, the girl transfers her love to the father, while the boy remains in love with his mother, and she ceases to fear him as a rival. He becomes an object of love. Third, for this and other reasons connected with the castration complex, she identifies herself with the mother and accepts the feminine role. As a result of all this she is not dominated by the fear that the father will destroy her, so she has no need to develop a strong super-ego. She is moved more by the need to love and be loved. Hence she does not acquire the strong inner acceptance of moral authority and the fear of transgressing moral principles which characterise the boy. The ego-ideal rather than the super-ego governs her moral thinking. She does not reach moral decisions by analysing the moral principles at stake, but by projecting herself into the situation and feeling her way to a solution. A woman is more practical and positive in her moral decisions than is a man because they are personal rather than abstract, and her judgements are intuitive rather than analytical. From the masculine point of view women are amoral and without conscience, and women see men as devious and usually blind to the obvious in moral matters.

What I have been describing so briefly is the normal process of growth. The so-called Oedipus complex is not an abnormality; to be fixed in it, not to grow through it, is the abnormality, that is, in the sense of failure of ideal development. Few, if any of us, manage the complete resolution of the complex necessary for complete personal growth.

We would not develop the internal authority and become moral beings if we did not enter into the conflict of desires which compels us to seek a solution. We develop the super-ego to enable us to control two impulses which have become dangerous, desire to possess the mother and desire to get rid of the father by destroying him. As Freud said, the primal sins are incest and parricide. But the desires were natural and perfectly normal when we held them. Not to hold them would be an indication of something seriously wrong. Hence a precondition of becoming a moral being is to have done something which our new moral sense must condemn as wrong. But we did not hold it to be wrong when we did it. We were in the age of innocence. Thus as soon as we have a moral sense it tells us that we have done wrong. The sense of having sinned is universal among normal people. This is one of the facts which the Fall is postulated to explain, but we must see it as a step in the forward growth of man. The age of innocence was not one free from sin, but one in which the categories of sin and wrongdoing did not apply.

What I have said does not mean that our moral health is to be measured by the severity of our self-condemnation, by the strength of the super-ego. The super-ego controls more than our moral standards; by repression it shelters the self, for instance, from shame and inadequacy, the fear of being unlovable. The super-ego can be distorted. It may develop inadequately, so as not to exercise enough control, and it may become too severe, clamping down too strongly on the desires of the self. So simple a factor as the stimulation in infancy of aggressive impulses, by illness or treatment at the hands of the mother vacillating between overemotional caressing, neglect, and harshness, may distort the images of the parents which are internalised as conscience. The severity of conscience, and, I suggest, its later educability, depend more on the emotional life of the infant than upon the moral teaching given to him. *"Moral education is no substitute for love."* [1]

A stern conscience is not the sign of true moral maturity. It may be the reverse. It may indicate the presence of strong repressions which have forced the self to a defensive reaction against them, a reaction which has become embodied in the character of the person concerned. It is also likely that the conscience function has drawn to itself a large measure of repressed aggression. The heaviest repression of the aggressive impulses occurs, as Melanie Klein showed, in the first year of life and is achieved by diverting half the aggression upon the other half, setting up a division in the self. The repressive aggression is later absorbed into the super-ego, increasing its severity. It may be basically unrelated to moral principles, being primarily a defence against a felt danger. Its effect is not merely to produce a stern conscience, it also results in a load of unconscious guilt, which may become displaced on to relatively innocuous actions or impulses.

The aspect of conscience which I have been describing is the negative one, that which tells us we have sinned, or which constantly is forbidding us to do something to which our impulses move us. It enshrines the 'Thou shalt not' of morality. This is what it came into existence to do. If it existed alone it would more or less paralyse us into inaction. The positive side of morals is more important, that which bids us do something, not from mere desire for satisfaction of pleasure, but because what is enjoined appears to have an absolute value. It is something we ought to do. It is the standard by which we measure our sins of omission.

It is a pity that the two forms of morality have been confused with each other. This is easy enough to understand, for when we have committed a sin of omission our self-condemnatory function takes over and accuses us of having done something wrong. But they come from different sources. The genesis of the super-ego is from fear, fear of the father primarily, but also including in it fear of the mother. Let us call the positive ideals of conduct the ego-ideal.

The sanction of the ego-ideal is love, not fear. It begins in infancy with the overwhelming desire of the infant to win his mother's love. He wants to do what will please her, for that intensifies his relationship with her. He comes to learn that certain things please her more than others, and as he grows older he learns more and more the kind of person she wants him to be or become. As Leslie Weatherhead pointed out, this learning is all too often hindered by the fact that she is more apt to say 'don't do that' than to give positive guidance. But the growing child tends to find that what his mother wants him to be conflicts with his own natural desires and leads to a struggle inside himself. His love of his mother and his need to be loved by her make him accept as desirable what she wants, but in fact he may find himself doing or being something else. There is a division inside him between the ideal he acknowledges and strives after and what he sees himself to be.

What he has learned from his mother is reinforced when he gets to know his father by his love and admiration for him, and even the rivalry with him can intensify the identification, for he sees his father as having full possession of the mother, which is what he wants. There grows in him the desire to be what his father is. Thus he sets up an ideal of what he wants to become, an ideal which of course embodies acceptance of the picture he forms of what they want him to be so as to keep their love. This picture is being constantly added to as he grows. He learns from his mates, from other people he admires, from his own reflections over the meaning of life. In the end the religious man centres his aspirations on God. Always, however, he will find his ideal unrealised. It grows as he grows. As he attains to one stage a further opens beyond him, so he must always be aware of the gap between what he is and what he wants to be; he must always fall short of his current ideal.

This inevitable gap between the real and the ideal self explains the sense of proneness to sin which underlies the doctrine of the Fall. Nothing we can do will close the gap, for the ideal ever recedes from the real. Again we note that this is a sign of healthy development and is the way in which we are stimulated to grow. It is not a sign of failure but of success. It is the spiritually creative element within us. If we give up the ideal it is because we have ceased to believe in love or to want it and we have cut ourselves off from effective communion with other people, unless, perhaps, we make hate a substitute for love.

The gap, too, explains why the great saints sincerely describe themselves as sinners. They are more aware of the gap than the ordinary man, just because they have a clearer vision of what man might be. The forgiveness they seek from God is the help which comes from him by his love, which both sustains the ideal and makes the quest worthwhile above everything else, makes it the meaning of one's being. This driving power of love is richer than the sanction of fear, fear of punishment, fear of the withdrawal of love. It is such a conviction of the supremacy and finality of love that is expressed by "While we were yet sinners, Christ died for us," and "Perfect love casteth out fear." With the development of the ego-ideal we move out of the realm of the obligation of duty to the empowering recognition and identification of the self with what is good in life.

This would be impossible if the Fall meant that we had dropped away from a pristine goodness. What seems to point to a fall is really a stage on the way to the fulfilment of God's destiny for man. Adam ate, the fruit of the tree of the knowledge of good and evil, and he became able to choose good deliberately and became more godlike in consequence.

CHAPTER 2 NOTES

1 D. W. Winnicott, *The Maturational Processes and the Facilitating Environment,* p. 97 (italics his).

3 MEANING AND MEANINGLESSNESS
IN RECENT LITERATURE

"The Theatre of the Absurd," Martin Esslin has said, "can be seen as the reflection of what seems to be the attitude most genuinely representative of our own time. The hallmark of this attitude is its sense that the certitudes and unshakeable basic assumptions of former ages have been swept away, that they have been tested and found wanting, that they have been discredited as cheap and somewhat childish illusions. The decline of religious faith was masked until the end of the Second World War by the substitute religions of faith in progress, nationalism and various totalitarian fallacies. All this was shattered by the war. By 1942, Albert Camus was calmly putting the question why, since life had lost all meaning, man should not escape in suicide." [1] Has life in fact lost all meaning? Do events, words, images any longer convey significance? Or are we constantly being driven back to the terrible conclusion that all is sound and fury, signifying nothing?

To attempt to define meaning seems an almost pointless exercise. From our earliest years we are all concerned with the establishing of some kind of orderliness within the constantly changing environment in which we find ourselves. By an extraordinarily complex and delicate process, patterns of sound become the grammar of language, patterns of light become the grammar of visual interchange. And out of the dialectic of verbal and visual interchange common understanding, common enjoyment, common anticipation mysteriously emerge. Meaning is not something that can be defined apart from the interchange. Only in relationship can personal life be sustained and only in communication can meaning be discovered.

But meaning is not only discovered: meaning can be celebrated. Meaning is discovered in its simplest terms when the child learns to associate a particular sound ('Dad') with a particular object. Meaning expands as the child expresses an emotion of delight or apprehension in relation to the father by employing the word 'Dad' in a particular way. And these two processes can continue indefinitely through life. Meaning is *discovered* when a certain formulation in verbal or imagistic form is understood to correspond to relatively stable or recurring patterns of experience in the external world. Meaning is *celebrated* when verbal or imagistic forms are constructed to correspond to relatively new or unusual experiences which stir the emotions and call to be expressed in some patterned way.

The celebration of meaning has come to be regarded as pre-eminently the work of the artist. He may use sounds or visual shapes, he may employ musical instruments or the human voice, inert materials or human gestures, but whatever his material he is endeavouring to communicate his own emotional experience through the medium of the fabrication which is his work of art. Yet he constantly finds himself in a dilemma. The experiences which he is anxious to communicate inevitably represent experiences of the past; in other words they contain elements of *oldness*. How then can the new be related to the old? How can the excitement of present realities be adequately celebrated by employing symbols derived from the past? This is the problem of meaning as it confronts the artist again and again.

In some ways the task of the writer, whether of novels or of the drama, is easier than that of the architect or the musical composer. The writer has words at his disposal all of which carry *some* meaning in the ordinary processes of social communication. He can be confident that *some* meaning will be conveyed by the words which he employs. But the urgent question for him is whether any words or combination of words can convey the experience which he is *most* anxious to celebrate. So there comes about the 'intolerable wrestle with words and meanings' with the constant frustration of only learning 'to get the better of words for the thing one no longer has to say'. He must try to communicate meaning: yet the meaning seized from his words is so often far removed from the experience which he is seeking to celebrate and convey.

Obviously in a time of rapid scientific and social change this problem becomes ever more acute. The new gains an increasing ascendancy over the old and the language of the past seems to have a diminishing relation to the experiences of the present. In addition the range of possible communication becomes ever wider and this in turn diminishes the number of common structures of life that the artist can take for granted. It is not surprising that the writer feels strongly tempted to emphasise inordinately the newness of the forms which he uses, even to search after the eccentric and idiosyncratic, in order to celebrate what he feels to be of major significance. At the same time he is tempted to remain content if a very limited number of what he comes to regard as informed and sensitive readers are prepared to respond to his own formulated vision. In other words the artist tends to gather to himself a severely limited coterie who can discern meaning in strange and esoteric experiences which to the vast majority are meaningless and absurd.

Examples of the tendencies which I have just noted may be found in the spate of novels which flow from the presses—each in its own way celebrating some limited aspects of human experience and making its appeal to a comparatively limited audience—or in the emergence of what has come to be called 'The Theatre of the Absurd' in which again limited audiences are entertained by what at least appear to be disconnected images and incoherent sentences assembled together in situations which seem trivial if not entirely meaningless. The intent of the artist in either case may be entirely serious. But so oppressed is he by the lack of relation between his own experience and the general patterns of society at large that he can see no way of transmitting his vision except by emphasising the bizarre, the paradoxical and even the absurd. The novel which illuminates the total gamut of human experience or the drama which finds universal meaning in some limited play of human words and actions seem almost to belong to a past age. The question arises whether any comprehensive statement about life's ultimate meaning can be conveyed through literary media such as the novel, the poem or the drama at the present time.

I believe that such images are not entirely lacking. Amidst the innumerable representations of the human condition which may be seen on the stage, on the television screen, on the printed page, occasionally a man stands out who seems in some mysterious way rock-like, yet tremendously dynamic, rooted in this world, yet not bound by this world, the grateful inheritor of the past yet ever straining towards the future, holding fast to an inner integrity yet constantly reaching out to his social environment. The artist who can create authentic figures of this kind seems to me to be speaking in a particularly significant way about our own predicament. We cannot return to a purely static image. At the same time we cannot find meaning in a mere flux of impressions. We want to see a man fully exposed to and grappling with the reality of his time; at the same time we want to see him achieving in and through the encounter an authentic and meaningful existence of his own.

It is because I believe that each of the authors on whom I am proposing to comment has given us a vision of such a man that I have selected them from amongst the great host of modern writers who in one way or another are seeking to throw light on the human situation through their art. I do not claim that any single figure in the plays of Arthur Miller or the novels of Patrick White stands out so pre-eminently that we are likely to say: 'There is real man, authentic man, essential man'—though a good case could be made for John Proctor amongst all the characters of the plays, and for Mordecai Himmelfarb amongst all the characters of the novels. Rather I am suggesting that a deepening acquaintance with the works of these two authors leads gradually to the heightening of one's awareness of what man can become in relation to his world, in relation to society, in relation to himself, in relation to the Divine. I shall look first at Miller's plays and in particular at *The Crucible*. I shall then look at White's novels and in particular at *Riders in the Chariot*.

Arthur Miller

A statement made by Miller in the course of an article written for *Harper's Magazine* in 1960 seems to me fundamental for the interpretation of his work. "I am simply asking for a theatre," he wrote, "in which an adult who wants to live can find plays that will heighten his awareness of *what living in our time involves*" [my italics]. His plays do not necessarily provide solutions. They do illuminate the issues which have assumed a particular form and prominence under modern conditions.

His earlier plays, *All my Sons* (1947) and *Death of a Salesman* (1949) might have given the impression that the problems of modern living, generated as they have been by war and technology and new business methods, are unlike any that belong to previous ages. But *The Crucible*, set in seventeenth-century New England, made clear that in Miller's view the form of the stresses and ambiguities and responsibilities may change but that certain fundamental issues have to be grappled with at all times and in all places. Of these, the chief is the age-long tension between determinism and the freedom of the individual to commit himself in responsible decision. Whatever form determinism may take—fate, the gods, heredity, a class structure, a system of government, an economic pattern—the question for the individual is whether he has any real freedom of movement at all and if so what are the limitations and restraints beyond which he may not hope to go.

The two earlier plays which I have mentioned employ a *family* situation to draw out the ambiguities of life. In *All my Sons* we see on the one side a typical ideal of American family relationships: the father successful in business, prepared to be ruthless where necessary in promoting efficiency, is always concerned to use the results of his own 'drive' for the benefit and enjoyment of his wife and family, and has his hopes set on the son who will write a still more impressive chapter in the success story which the father has begun. On the other side we see a business subordinate trampled on, a lie and a sham covered up, a son estranged, a daughter torn between conflicting loyalties, a wife driven to living in a world of illusion, a final escape through the forbidden door of suicide. The play was designed, Miller says, to bring the central figure Joe Keller "into the direct path of the consequences he had wrought". If this could be done convincingly, it would provide at least one man's testimony to the fact that we live in a moral world and that no man can simply walk away from his activities in the world at large into the final security of his own family circle. 'Business' may seem to be a closed circle, a self-perpetuating mechanism with its own standards of efficiency against which no man may rebel. It is Joe Keller's son, Chris, who, by his initial readiness to renounce the security of the family business at any cost, sets in train a series of events which leads to tragedy but to an ultimate cleansing of the moral atmosphere and to a personal release of creative personal energies.

Death of a Salesman leaves behind all war associations and explores more fully the world of big business which for long had been the key feature of American life. Willy Loman is a salesman, a very ordinary salesman, a minor cog in the great business machine. He has had reasonable success, enough to buy his own house and car and the gadgets regarded as essential for modern family life. But his whole existence is concentrated upon the advancement of his two boys. He shares their interests, their games, their hopes, their arguments. He slaves for them, dreams for them and finally sacrifices himself for them. He must be a 'success' in the only way known to him—that of a salesman—in order that he may vindicate his own existence and have something of value to hand over to the next generation. He constantly looks back to the past and to his own inheritance from his father. The *summum bonum* as far as he is concerned is to hand over something of a similar kind to his sons.

But his sons want to go their own way. They see through the father's philosophy of life which is in fact an evasion of reality. He never comes to know who he really is. He is simply a middle man, a salesman, always on the move, having no fixed relationships, constructing nothing permanent. In reality he has nothing to hand on.

"Willy was a salesman." (His neighbour Charley is speaking in the Requiem.) "And for a salesman there is no rock bottom to the life. He don't put a bolt to a nut, he don't tell you the law or give you medicine. He's a man way out there in the blue, riding on a smile and a shoeshine. And when they start not smiling back—that's an earthquake." Willy is driven forward all his life by the passion to succeed, even in a minor job of a great impersonal business house. He never knows himself or his own real capacities. He never really knows his sons or understands their problems. Only in and through his final action of self-destruction does he achieve a certain authenticity and release new forces which mysteriously enable his sorrowing wife to cry: "We're free."

In *A View from the Bridge* the setting for the working out of dramatic conflict is the kin-group rather than the single family. Within this group—a society of Sicilian peasants living on the New York waterfront with their firmly held moral and social taboos—the most important source of conflict is the awakening desire of the younger generation to relate itself to the life of the wider society by which it is surrounded. This arouses in Eddie, the central figure, feelings of possessiveness, jealousy, blind hatred. He reaches the point of betraying even one of his own kin and the tragedy of revenge plays itself out to a finish. But there is something heroic about Eddie. He is not just the little man who is always ready to settle for half. He refuses simply to swim with the tide and to allow all intimate loyalties to be swallowed up within the conformities of a great society. He is deeply frustrated. He strikes out madly, unforgivably. Yet he retains his own individual dignity. He will preserve his 'name', his final identity at all costs, even the cost of his own death. Like Joe Keller and Willy Loman, Eddie Carbone dies a death which somehow redeems the mistakes and frustrations and self-deceptions of his life. In Miller's words he refuses to settle for half but instead allows himself to be wholly known. His life ends in tragedy but that, in Miller's scale of values, is better than to "return, again and again and again, to the pathetic swampland where the waters are old tears and not the generating seas from which new kinds of life arise".

I might refer to *A Memory of Two Mondays* in which a boy, seemingly a very ordinary boy, determines to break through the artificialities and the aimlessness of his environment in a business house, to rise above necessity and to discover meaning through an action which on the face of it seems absurd. But by general consent Miller's greatest play is *The Crucible*, the one instance in which he has chosen to throw a searchlight on contemporary problems and issues by reconstructing a situation and a series of social events which happened nearly three centuries ago. There was a system of iron conformity in Salem under a supposedly divine law, just as, Miller believes, there is a system of iron conformity today under a supposedly divine revelation of what constitutes the American way of life. Any deviation now, as then, is visited with the direst penalties. But deviations do not normally arise in any simple and straightforward fashion. There may be some *private* failing or indulgence which haunts a man's conscience and makes him wonder if he dare take a stand on a question of *public* morality. There may be some special manifestations within the body public which may cause the social code to be enforced even more impersonally and inexorably than it was before. How can the individual hope to make his protest when all is so complex and so heavily weighted against him?

Miller explores this complex situation through his central character John Proctor, a courageous, hard-headed and responsible citizen whose unsatisfied sexual longings have found an outlet in an affair with his wife's serving-maid. When revulsion comes and he renounces the liaison, the girl becomes leader of a hysterical conspiracy to entrap Elizabeth Proctor, the wife. Thereupon John himself is thrown into a state of acute conflict between the remembrance of his guilty past and the determination to resist the absurdities of the panic of the community with its consequent witch hunt. The sustained tension, the personal dialogue, the conflict of values are brilliantly worked out and John Proctor emerges as the tragic hero who is prepared to endure the final rejection by his own society if only he can preserve his 'name', his authentic identity, his existence as an individual standing for ultimate truth rather than for the traditions and regulations and conformities of a false system, however venerable and all-embracing it might seem to be.

The play throws into high relief two issues on which Miller feels passionately. The first is man's temptation at all times and in all places to hand over his conscience. Just because moral conflict is always painful, just because man can never be certain of his own ability to judge moral issues rightly, he is tempted again and again to hand over his conscience and leave necessary decisions to some corporate authority—church, state, party, public opinion—who will act on his behalf. The second is man's difficulty at all times of discerning just where the forces of disintegration in his social environment are to be located. As Miller has said: "Most American dramas revolve round the victimisation of the hero by inhuman forces of society but these evil forces have become so pervasive and ill-defined that we are left with a hero whose enemies are invisible." It is comparatively easy to establish a code in which black is on one side and white on the other and no place is allowed for the 'fuddled afternoon' in which goodness is mixed with evil. But life is not just an inert mass of experience to be dissected in this way. Only by a constant process of probing and testing and comparing can man locate the seat of infection at any particular time. The plague is never finally extinguished. Every new generation must be prepared to search for and deal radically with the particular manifestation of evil in its own time.

Few playwrights have written so frankly and so forcefully about the characters and the conflicts of their plays as has Miller. "I am trying to define," he has said, "what a human being should be, how he can survive in today's society, without having to appear to be a different person from what he basically is." And what alarms him above all else in today's society is the cult of efficiency with, as its necessary corollary, what Hensley Henson once called 'the lust for uniformity'. "The question must begin to be asked," Miller says, "not whether a thing will work or pay, not whether it is more efficient than its predecessor, more popular and more easily accepted: but what will it do to human beings?" It is the same concern that his fellow-countryman Robert Lowell expressed when asked what he thought of the modern situation: "I think," he said, "the thing Pasternak expressed is universal—that is the danger of the great impersonal bureaucratic machine rolling over everything and flattening out humanity."

This does not mean that Miller has his head in the sand and objects to machinery or efficiency as such. Nor does it mean that he would have the individual withdraw from the larger society and attempt to work out some kind of solitary salvation. Rather it means that he is aware of man being subjected in the modern world to subtle pressures and unconscious influences more powerful than ever before towards the implementation of the model of the smoothly efficient machine, the social mechanism in which everything and everyone is geared to the following of a well-defined path towards a well-defined goal. In a sense there is no escape from this process and this determinism. Yet it is Miller's final affirmation that there is a paradox of the individual will, there is a point beyond which man can refuse to be 'measured and systematically accounted for'. In other words man is 'more than the sum of his stimuli'. He is an exception to his environment however much he may be a creature of it.

It is the supreme object of the plays to show how this paradox of *the more, the exceptional* (or as I would like to express it, the transcendent) can be actually realised in life. It can become evident to the world, it can become real to a man himself, only through some crisis of commitment, the moment when he ventures all for the identification of his 'name'. (The reference to the 'name' is one of the most characteristic of Miller's symbolic forms.) He writes: "Time, characterisations, and other elements are treated differently from play to play, but all to the end that that moment of commitment be brought forth, that moment when, in my eyes, a man differentiates himself from every other man, that moment when out of a sky full of stars he fixes on one star."

To some this may appear to be nothing more than a cry of despair in face of an inexorable, deterministic world. At least it is *a cry* and perhaps our time is such that it is the voice crying in the wilderness that we most need to hear. Moreover, if Bonamy Dobrée is right when he affirms that "The end of tragedy is to show the dignity of man for all his helpless littleness in the face of the universe, for all his nullity under the blotting hand of time," then I think that Miller may be said to have created a modern form of tragedy in which such very 'ordinary' characters as Willy Loman and John Proctor and Eddie Carbone attain true dignity and greatness in the moment of their final commitment to a value greater than life itself.

Patrick White

When Patrick White's novel *Riders in the Chariot* was published, *The Times Literary Supplement* entitled an article reviewing his total achievement up to that date: 'Attempting the Infinite.' Actually the title was taken from one of Mr. White's own books in which the central character Voss is concerned 'to discard the inessential and attempt the infinite'. But it seems to me that the summing-up was apt and justified. White has never been satisfied with the ephemeral, the partial, the inessential. From the time of the appearance of his first novel *Happy Valley* in 1939 to the year of the publication of *Riders in the Chariot* he was constantly moving forwards in his exploration of the heights and the depths, the achievements and the failures, the emptiness and the significance of human existence. Maybe this resulted in books which tended to be overintense and overserious. But it certainly did not result in works lacking interest and marks of deep insight and compassion. The total interpretation of man which emerges is worthy of the most careful attention.

His earlier novels are concerned with such questions as the place of suffering in human life, what is the criterion of being truly alive, how to distinguish between reality and illusion. At length he was ready to tackle a more comprehensive theme. In 1956 a novel with the significant title *The Tree of Man* appeared, in 1957 *Voss* and in 1961 the most widely embracing of all, *Riders in the Chariot*. In these books he is concerned with nothing less than the nature and destiny of man, his potentialities for good and evil, for littleness and greatness, for the trivial and the transcendent. The place of religion is not obtruded but neither is it excluded. In fact it would be hard to deny that in the last resort Mr. White finds satisfaction only in an essentially religious interpretation of human existence.

History seems to suggest that there is always the possibility for literature to be reborn within the context of a new geographical environment when writers sufficiently steeped in an older tradition have the courage to relate themselves wholeheartedly to the new. This could be illustrated from the creative works of Hebrew prophets in exile (not least from Ezekiel whose symbolism was to prove so appealing to White himself), from the novels of English authors who exposed themselves fully to the influences of a particular region, from the writings of Melville and Hawthorne, Faulkner and Warren on the North American continent and most recently of all from White in Australia. He was born in Australia but the fact that he was educated in England meant that he became deeply involved in the cultural and literary traditions of the 'old' country and his earlier works are largely set in the established world of the West. But *The Tree of Man* marks a significant change. Not only has the author returned to Australia; he has gone back to the beginnings, back to man faced with the possibilities of a new start, back, as it were, to the Australian Adam confronted with the task of clearing the bush and bringing some semblance of order into the primitive chaos of this new land. It is the re-enactment of Eden and the Fall, of the beginnings of human achievement and of human perversity, in a new environment, under new conditions. Are there evidences that the shoots from the parent stock will be disease-free in this new setting? Or to put it in another way, is the saga of man likely to reveal altogether different features when its background is the interior of a virgin continent?

In a revealing moment of self-disclosure White once said: "Because the void I had to fill was so immense, I wanted to try to suggest in this book [that is, *The Tree of Man*] every possible aspect of life, through the lives of an ordinary man and woman. But at the same time I wanted to discover the extraordinary behind the ordinary, the mystery and the poetry which alone could make bearable the lives of such people and incidentally my own since my return" [that is, to Australia]. Stan and Amy Parker, the Australian

Adam and Eve, are very ordinary people. They love one another but never reach the depths of understanding one another; they bear children, one of whom gains an empty worldly security, the other of whom ends in an equally empty violent death; they experience temptation, disappointment, the pleasures of the simplicities of the world of nature, the strains of their contacts with the unrealities of city life; but they never gain fulfilment through the sense of any comprehensive meaning or purpose being worked out in the succession of the days and the progress of the years. A recurring symbol is the symbol of emptiness. Life has brought many satisfactions; in clearing the forest, in building the home, in planting the garden, in stocking the farm. But all this is not enough. There is a mystery undisclosed, an emptiness unfilled, a love unrealised. Only at the end—of the book, of the life of Stan Parker—is there the glimpse of life's unity and resolution in the vision of the One who is 'answer to all sums'.

If *The Tree of Man* is dominantly passive—man's emptiness waiting to be filled—*Voss* is tremendously active—man's ambition straining to subdue a continent. It was Nietzsche who claimed that two aspects of man were equally represented in human mythology. On the one hand man is seen (as in the Adam story) as weak, self-indulgent, an easy prey to seduction, craven and fearful after the perpetration of some forbidden act. On the other hand he appears (as in the Babel story) as proud, self-assertive, determined to scorn all obstacles in his progress to the heights, sullen and rebellious if thwarted in any of his projects. And it is, I think, a mark of White's stature that he does not settle for any single and uniform interpretation of the human drama. There is the man close to nature in sympathy and sensitivity; there is the man dominating nature by experimentation and organisation. There is the woman who is practical, patient, preoccupied with the demands of the home and the children and their surroundings; there is the woman who is ardent, ready to sacrifice herself for spiritual ends, rich in inner resources and insights. Voss has supreme self-confidence, and believes that every natural phenomenon can be brought under man's control. Laura, the woman of the story, is also self-confident, believing that her imagination can enter unerringly into the minds of others and detect the innermost secrets of their hearts. Voss is determined to prove that he can penetrate to the heart of every structure of the natural world; Laura is sure that she can penetrate to the heart of every structure of the human imagination.

The story follows man and woman, through the suffering and travail appropriate to each, to a final redemption in which they find themselves united in humility and in a profound relationship of the spirit though not of the body. Voss perishes in the midst of what Ted Hughes has called 'the blindingly bright and utterly dark power of the Australian desert'. Laura is united with him in the midst of a delirious fever, during which she herself experiences the darkest night of dereliction though her physical self is spared. Each is revealed at the beginning of the novel as possessing a contempt for God, Voss because God is *not* in his own image, Laura because God *is* in her own image. Each comes finally to faith, Voss as he learns that he is not God, Laura as she learns that her life can only attain fulfilment as she becomes united with the suffering of God.

The comprehensive interpretation of human existence which White was approaching through *The Tree of Man* and *Voss* was finally, it seems, achieved in *Riders in the Chariot*. The canvas is broader. More characters are involved. Good and evil are revealed more clearly in their perennial conflict. Jew and Christian, industrial man and the aborigine, the intellectual and the man of action, the traditional and the modern, the puritan and the sensualist are brought together in a fascinating structure of interrelationships which finds a unifying point of reference in a vision which transcends all human ambitions and conflicts and binds together in a spiritual fellowship men and women of every place and of every time.

The story is built around the lives of four characters representing, it would appear at first sight, utterly different realms of experience. There is a female recluse clinging to one of the great houses, built by a successful early Australian settler, but which is now little more than a monument to a dead past. There is a Jewish refugee from central Europe, once a leading figure in academic circles, who escaped almost miraculously from the Nazi tyranny and finally emigrated to the Southern Continent. Thirdly there is a woman who left England as a simple country girl and found herself at length married to a brute of a man and responsible for the maintenance of a large family, a task which she fulfilled by slaving at the wash-tub and by strengthening herself in her vision of the triumph of God. Finally there is a vivid but elusive figure, an aborigine who had been introduced to the Christian tradition by pioneering missionaries but who was quite unprepared to cope with the temptations and perplexities of city life. Here are four types, reminiscent of the four elemental constituents of the universe, earth, air, water, fire, all drawn together by the fact that they share a single vision and are finally united in a common experience.

White captivates the reader by the skill with which he depicts important scenes in the lives of each of these characters. His novel, it has been suggested, is like a searchlight swinging its beam right across Australia (but also across sections of England and Germany and Israel), shedding a brief light on aristocrats and factory hands, on scholars and peasants, on suburbia and the Australian out-back. But though brief it is never dim. The light penetrates to the depths and constantly invites the questions: What do all these outward manners and social manifestations and laboured organisations really amount to? What was the outcome of National Socialism? What is likely to be the end of the Jewish State? What is the purpose of life in the factories and suburbs of a great modern city? White's searchlight is pitiless in exposing the hypocrisies and shams and falsehoods of the human scene. Few escape its exposure and its question—the avowedly religious as well as the unbeliever, the upholder of moral standards as well as the open sensualist. Yet though he exposes he does not presume to judge. And the exposure of the sham and the trivial only serves to throw into stronger relief the revelation of the authentic and the real.

There can be no doubt that for White human life gains stability and depth only if it is related to that which is beyond human description or determination, that which gives man power to endure when all the circumstances of life—hereditary, social, political—seems to be against him. It would be hard to imagine a more motley collection—the half-crazy love-starved spinster, the highly sophisticated, spiritually sensitive Jew, the poverty-stricken simple-minded washerwoman, the emotionally explosive, physically disintegrating aborigine. Yet each endures 'as seeing Him Who is invisible'. Each sees the Chariot of Fire at critical moments of illumination, the chariot which Ezekiel the prophet celebrated through a rich confusion of imagery and which has remained a powerful and moving symbol of Divine energy, both in Jewish and Christian symbolism, since his time. Miss Hare sees it in the glory of the sunset, Himmelfarb in his study in an exalted flash of illumination, Mrs. Godbold at her wash-tub as she sings of the King riding in the clouds, Dubbo as he reads Ezekiel's words and tries to express them through the glowing colours of his palette. In a strange way these four *become* the four living creatures of the vision. They are transfigured in the 'chariot-sociable' until their souls illuminate their bodies and their humanity attains beatitude in the vision of God.

Patrick White has asked the great questions about man in a new way by formulating them in terms of man's experience of a new continent. What is permanent in the midst of flux? (*The Tree of Man*). What is the deepest truth of man's (and woman's) existence? (*Voss*). By what symbol (or constellation of symbols) can man transcend the immediate and experience the eternal, the ultimately real? (*Riders in the Chariot*). Other questions arise in the course of his work—who are the living and who the dead, what is illusion and what reality, what is success and what failure—but White can be content with nothing less than the discovery of a clue to the complexity of man's total relationship with the infinite. Call it the Transcendent, the Other, the One, what we will, White affirms that unless man has found his point of reference for individual and social life in the Beyond, in that which lies outside the ordinary and the manageable and the predictable, he is bound fast to a wheel of existence which has neither goal nor meaning. The Chariot is an elusive but a compelling symbol. Through the fires of suffering man ascends. The Blessed are those who find no final satisfaction on earth but ride in the Chariot of Redemption beyond the sunset into the true glory.

Having sketched the contribution which these two writers have made to the problem of meaning in our contemporary world, I offer in conclusion the following reflections.

First, it seems to me that Arthur Miller is constantly seeking to move from the circumference of life to its centre. He is prepared to fasten upon a comparatively minor series of incidents in a social situation and to use them as a means of leading in to the very heart of human existence—to the struggle which every man must make to discover his particular identity, to the commitment which every man must make in order to establish his right to be in the world at all. Writing about *Death of a Salesman* Miller says that it grew above all from "the image of a need greater than hunger or sex or thirst, a need to leave a thumbprint somewhere on the world. A need for immortality, and by admitting it, the knowing that one has carefully inscribed one's name on a cake of ice on a hot July day". If this is indeed a universal need, then in spite of so much in the world that seems meaningless, the artist can, by relating his new vision to this age-long 'drive', celebrate meaning in a way which at any moment of time can stretch out towards a universality of appeal.

Secondly, it seems to me that Patrick White tends to work in the opposite direction. Beginning with man and woman in a new situation, in a new territory, he stretches out along the fourfold axes of space and time to embrace the totality of human existence. Stan and Amy in the Australian virgin land represent man and woman in a similar situation of new beginnings at any point in history; Voss and Laura journeying into the interior, physically and imaginatively, represent man and woman concerned with life's adventures and quests at all periods of time; Himmelfarb and Dubbo, Miss Hare and Mrs. Godbold, in their relationships with one another within a more complex meeting of nations and cultures and technologies represent again the meetings which have been taking place down through the ages and which have attained a world-wide significance at the present time. White does not discount the trivialities and the waste, the refusals and the treacheries, the unexpected falls and the tragic failures. And yet the framework of the fourfold cross, mandala,[2] co-ordinate axes, symbolising a total embrace and an ultimate reconciliation, can be seen through the tangled maze of all these distortions. Meaning can still be celebrated even when drunken irresponsibility crucifies moral integrity on an old jacaranda tree.

My final comment on these two writers has been suggested to me by a profoundly interesting passage in Eric Bentley's book *The Life of the Drama*. At the conclusion of his chapter on the place of thought and ideas in the theatre he asks in effect whether there is any single word which better than another expresses the aim and object of playwriting. Is thought (theme, idea) the drama's true end? Or a philosophy of life? Or wisdom? After considering these various possibilities he turns instead to the word *vision*.

"Vision," he writes, "is a better word, and gathering together the threads, we might say: a play [and I would equally affirm a novel] presents a vision of life, and to the idea of vision the idea of wisdom naturally adheres. To share this vision and this wisdom—just as naturally—is not to receive information or counsel but rather to have a 'momentous experience'. The momentousness is to be defined partly in emotional terms: according to the play in question there accrues joy, elation, exaltation, ecstasy or whatever. But an essential part of our conviction that such an experience is momentous derives from what we take to be the import of the play.

"Finally, if part of this conviction derives from what the play means, another part derives from the mere fact *that* it means. Meaningfulness is itself momentous for human beings, as they discover *a contrario*, whenever life has no meaning for them. *All art serves as a lifebelt to rescue us from the ocean of meaninglessness*[3]—an extraordinary service to perform at any time and more than ever today when religion and philosophy prove less and less able to perform it. To be thus rescued is to rediscover our personal dignity, through which alone we can discover dignity in others, dignity in human life as such. And attendant upon our sense of human dignity is a sense of what Goethe beautifully called 'the dignity of significance'."[4]

Vision and dignity are words which I find wholly appropriate as I reflect upon the art of Miller and White. A vision of meaningful human existence does emerge from their writings. And it is a vision in which man emerges as a creature of dignity whenever his life becomes significant by reason of its relationship to the Other, the More, the Beyond, the Ultimate, however we care to name or express it. Neither Miller nor White could be called an explicitly Christian writer. But each in his own way bears witness to the Transcendent and it is only where there is some, even faint, recognition of the dimension of transcendence that any witness to Christ as the revelation of God in human terms begins to make sense.

CHAPTER 3 NOTES

1. Martin Esslin, *The Theatre of the Absurd*, p. 16.
2. In this assessment of White's interpretation of human existence I have made no reference to *The Solid Mandala* (1966). While recognising the brilliant characterisation of the twin brothers I have found it difficult to sustain interest in the dreariness of their conversation and their surroundings. After *Riders in the Chariot* it is hard to avoid the feeling of anti-climax.
3. My italics.
4. Eric Bentley, *The Life of the Drama*, p. 146 ff.

4 EDWIN MUIR AND THE PREDICAMENT OF MAN

"Everything's good," said Kurilov.

"Everything?"

"Everything. Man is unhappy because he doesn't know he's happy. It's only that. That's all, that's all! If anyone finds out he'll become happy at once, that very minute—It's all good. I discovered it all of a sudden."

"But what about the man, the man who dies of hunger, or the man who insults and rapes the little girl, is that good too?"

"Yes, it is. And if anyone blows his brains out for the baby, that's good too. And if anyone doesn't that's good too. It's good for all those who know that all's good. If they knew it was good for them, it would be good for them, but as long as they don't know it's good for them, it will not be good for them. That's my idea in a nutshell—all of it—there isn't any other."

Dostoievsky was obsessed with the problems of good and evil, and so were the characters he created. This dialogue from *The Devils* gives one extreme answer. The other extreme is in *The Brothers Karamazov* when Ivan says to his brother Alyosha:

"'All these are problems [about whether God exists] which are entirely unsuitable to a mind created with the idea of only three dimensions. And so I accept God, and I accept him not only without reluctance, but what's more I accept his divine wisdom and his purpose—which are completely beyond our comprehension. I believe in the underlying order and meaning of life. I believe in the eternal harmony into which we are all supposed to merge one day. I believe in the "Word" to which the universe is striving and which itself was "with God" and which was God, and so on and so forth, *ad infinitum*. Many words have been bandied about on this subject. So it would seem I'm on the right path—or am I? Anyway you'd be surprised to learn, I think, that in the final result I refuse to accept this world of God's, and though I know that it exists, I absolutely refuse to admit its existence. Please understand, it is not God that I do not accept, but the world he has created. I do not accept God's world and I refuse to accept it. Let me put it another way: I am convinced like a child that the wounds will heal and their traces will vanish away, that all the offensive and comical spectacle of human contradictions will vanish like a pitiful image, like a horrible and odious invention of the feeble and infinitely puny Euclidean mind of man, and that in the world's finale, at the moment of eternal harmony, something so precious will happen and come to pass that it will suffice for all hearts, that it will allay all bitter resentments, that it will atone for all men's crimes, all the blood they have shed. It will suffice not only for the forgiveness but also for the justification done and come to pass, but I don't accept it and I won't accept it. Let even the parallel lines meet, and let me see them meet myself— I shall see and I shall say that they've met, but I still won't accept it . . . Listen: If all have to suffer so as to buy eternal harmony by their suffering, what have the children to do with it—tell me please? It is entirely incomprehensible why they too should have to suffer and why they should have to buy harmony by their sufferings. Why should they too be used as dung for someone's future harmony? . . . I shall perhaps myself cry aloud with the rest, as I look at the mother embracing her child's torturer, "Thou art just O Lord!" But I don't want to cry aloud then. While there's still time, I make haste to arm myself against it, and that is why I renounce higher harmony altogether . . . And therefore I hasten to hand back my ticket . . .'"

The views expressed by these two Dostoievsky characters are in the end the only two possible answers to the enigma of the goodness of God and the fact of evil rampant on a planet of his creation. Job had one solution and Julian of Norwich, with the advantage of Christian faith, another and profounder one, rather like that of Kurilov. 'The final and only alternative is that of Ivan Karamazov.

Poets and novelists, philosophers and theologians have striven with
this perennial and intransigent problem. The present age is obsessed
with it. Perhaps Teilhard de Chardin in *The Future of Man*, by the
use of his scientific knowledge, Christian faith, and lively imaginative intelligence has got as near as anyone to an explanation in his
attempt to show how the time–space totality of Evolution can be
justified and, indeed, made lovable. Kurilov turns out to be almost
right, and Ivan curiously and elaborately wrong.

Many of our own contemporary poets have entered deeply into
the sufferings and tribulations of humanity. Few have done so as
profoundly and unobtrusively as Edwin Muir. He was born in 1888
and died in 1959. He was deeply concerned with the problems
of evil and suffering, with man and his true nature, with time and
immortality—in fact with all the major themes discussed in this
book. Approaching them as a poet with a deep knowledge of himself
born of much suffering, much happiness, and an introspective
habit, he was able to throw light on the tortuous hopes and aspirations of human beings in their search for truth and desire for goodness, in a universe apparently indifferent and hopelessly ambivalent.
His conclusions are contained in his autobiography, two books of
literary criticism, and his collected poems. In these four books there
is wisdom and sensitive insight which amounts to spiritual genius.
In the end, in spite of terrible experiences after a very happy childhood and because of moments of intense happiness spasmodically
and inexplicably appearing in the tatterdemalion Euclidean world,

> Acceptance and gratitude
> Like travellers return
> And stand where first they stood.[2]

When he was five or six years old Muir saw for the first time a
heron standing on the far edge of the pond below his house. As it
flew away he was filled with fear and wonder at the gleaming grey
bird, and the very name heron had a strange significance. Later he
had a dream. "In the dream," he says in his autobiography, "I was
walking with some people when I saw a shining grey bird in a field.
I turned and said in an awed voice 'It's a heron.' We went towards it,

but as we came nearer it spread its tail like a peacock, so that we could see nothing else. As the tail grew I saw it was not round, but square, an impenetrable grey hedge of feathers; and at once I knew that its body was not a bird's body now, but an animal's, and that behind that gleaming hedge it was walking away from us on four feet padded like a leopard's or a tiger's. Then, confronting it in the field, there appeared an ancient dirty earth-coloured animal with a head like that of an old sheep or a mangy dog. Its eyes were soft and brown, it was alone against the splendid-tailed beast; yet it stood its ground, and prepared to fight the danger coming towards it, whether that was death, or merely humiliation and pain. From their look, I could see that the two animals knew each other, that they had fought a countless number of times, and after this battle would fight again, that each meeting would be the first meeting, and that the dark patient animal would always win. I did not see the fight, but I knew it would be ruthless and shameful, with a meaning of some kind perhaps, but no comfort."

Later, Muir reflected on the meaning of this extraordinary experience in *The Combat*—a poem 'inexhaustible and universal in effect', in Mr. Michael Hamburger's words. It is a spontaneous recreation of this childhood experience and the dream—a vision of strong dominating evil fighting weak but invincible good—the ever-recurring struggle, always inconclusive, never a victory for evil, and also never a final defeat of weak and vulnerable good. "This particular poem," continues Mr. Hamburger, "is one of the closest approximations in poetry to Kafka's world of absolute fiction . . . In comparison, even myth seems an impure form, too much tied to historical and local associations."

It is a record of an experience, with no questions asked, no conclusions indicated. As David Jones says in *Anathemata*: "For the artists the question is 'Does it?' rather than 'Ought it?'" No one creates or invents the problems which bite into human existence, but previous experience and present belief or unbelief and a passionate longing to find out will make each artist more sensitive to some of them. And one which we are specially concerned with is the problem of evil.

F

"Our first intuition of the world," Muir writes in his autobiography, "expands into vaster and vaster images, creating a myth which we act almost without knowing it, while our outward life goes on in its ordinary routine of eating, drinking, sleeping, working and making money in order to beget sons and daughters who will do the same . . . It is clear that we extend far beyond any boundary line which we can set for ourselves in the past or in the future, and that the life of every man is an endlessly repeated performance of the life of man. It is clear for the same reason that no autobiography can confine itself to conscious life, and that sleep, in which we pass a third of our existence, is a mode of experience, and our dreams a part of reality. In themselves our conscious lives may not be particularly interesting. But what we are not and can never be, our Fable, seems to me unconceivably interesting. I should like to write that Fable, but I cannot even live it; and all I could do if I related the outward course of my life would be to show how I have deviated from it; though even that is impossible since I do not know the Fable or anyone who knows it. One or two stages in it I can recognise: the age of innocence and the Fall and all the dramatic consequences which issue from the Fall. But those lie behind experience, not on its surface; they are stages in the Fable."

Muir's poetry is a constant attempt to find the Fable behind the Story, to find the eternal within the deviations and bewilderments and apparent insignificance of human life as it is lived in time. His main themes are: Loss of innocence, Eden, Childhood; Evil and the Fall; Time; Life as a journey, The labyrinth, Transfiguration. These are the themes with which all contributors to this work are concerned.

Loss of Innocence

Muir had an extremely happy childhood on a farm on one of the Orkneys, the Island of Wyre. He lived then, he says, "not in time ('for time still sat on the wrist of each day with its wings folded') but in a vast boundless calm . . . That world was a perfectly solid world, for the days did not undermine it but merely rounded it, or rather repeated it as if there were only one day endlessly rising and setting. Our first childhood is the only time in our lives when we exist within immortality, and perhaps all our ideas of immortality are influenced by it . . . We think and feel and believe immortally in our first few years, simply because time does not exist for us. We pay no attention to time, until he tugs us by the sleeve or claps his policeman's hand on our shoulder." At the age of eight the paradisial condition began to dissolve. The death of his parents and of a brother and sister, the unhappy and frustrating life and work in Glasgow caused him acute suffering. He became depressed and unhappy. Indeed it was not till his marriage in 1919 and his being psychoanalysed that he began to recover his losses and to probe the meaning, if any, of his life and the meaning, if any, of the universe, and to recapture the liveliness and freshness of his original vision of the world.

All his poems are reflections on his experience—tracing the Fable in the Story. To the child the Fable is credible and congenial. He has no experience to go on and he has not lost his initial confidence in the universe. He stands with one foot in Eden from which 'springs the root as clean as on the starting day'. But experience shatters this trust and makes it look infantile and absurd. In the poem *The Young Princes* Muir looks back to this age of innocence which he sees as a stage in every human life. Dylan Thomas in the poem of his own childhood, *Fern Hill*, also uses the Eden story to describe the ecstasy of childhood.

The age of innocence for both these poets was childhood and its experiences, in which, according to Muir, 'there is a completer harmony of all things with each other than he will ever know again'. The condition of the world and the inexplicability of man to himself or to others contrasted violently and painfully with the previous childhood state. Both poets felt a sense of irreparable loss and were appalled by it, and found here a description of every man's consciousness and this sense of guilt and alienation. It is a common but forgotten theme, and to Pascal was a proof of man's potential greatness. "The greatness of man," he says, "is even proved by his wretchedness. For what in animals we call nature, in man we call wretchedness; by which we recognise that his nature being now like that of the animals, he has fallen from a better nature which once was his. For who is unhappy at not being a king except a deposed king?"

Up to quite lately, the myth of the lost paradise was believed to be an historical fact. There was a Garden of Eden, Adam and Eve were the first parents. Their fall involved all their descendants in disaster. This is no longer credible. But the Fable still tells the truth. Muir and people like him who had a happy and secure childhood tend to look back to the innocence, exuberance, and trustfulness of that time and to deplore its loss. "Ah what a paradise begins with life," said John Clare, "and what a wilderness the knowledge of world discloses." Others have no past to feel nostalgic about, but they dislike the present and long for a future paradise. Both kinds of people bear witness to the fact of the unnaturalness of their present ambivalent state. The first remember the trust and confidence in the universe—represented by their parents—and wish for its restoration. The second look forward to a time when it is clear that the universe is friendly and on the side of their deepest and best aspirations. Both agree that the present is not what it should be, and that to acquiesce in it and become at home in it would be a betrayal. Both, by their discontent, bear witness to the fact that man is not an animal delighting in the temporal order as it is, nor an angel rejoicing in the eternal order as it was and is and always will be, but a being in transit, betwixt and between, where all is in the making. And that these aspirations are valid, for, us Teilhard de Chardin points out, one cannot accept the absurd position that the human soul is so badly devised that it contradicts within itself its own profoundest aspirations.

Evil and the Fall

In his essay on Chapman entitled *Royal Man*, Muir says of the play *The Tragedy of Bussy d'Ambois*: "We accept this hero and this drama as real because with one part of him man still lives in this world before the Fall, and with another after it; since the Fall— assuming that it stands for anything in human experience—is not

a historical event but something which is always happening."
Looking back it is rarely possible to point to any one event when the
traveller began to lose his way. Chance 'that turns the tale to grief
or joy' or Holy Luck, or 'what's given you by bold casual time' seem
to provide ambiguous signposts which men follow or are faintly
directed by,

> Yet as they travelled on, for many days
> These words rang in their ears as if they said,
> 'There was another road you did not see'.[3]

But though life is confusing and grace intermittent, the other part
of man which lives after the Fall and is entirely contained in the
time-space framework, is not just a passive instrument in the hands
of external forces. The royal road leads to an incomparable splendour, the trumpets and drums and banners which the children see,
the 'prescribed orientation' of man towards goodness in the Eden
story, are not lost or unheard merely through their empirical ambiva-
lence or questionable reality. They are clear enough and loud enough
at certain times to make them eternally trustworthy and their denial
a betrayal. There is a great gap between the certainty and clarity of
innocence and the apparently inevitable doubts and hesitations of
normal human existence. This gap is occasionally bridged. The
Fable shines through the Story. Sometimes the contrast seen on
looking back is painful. In a poem entitled *The Brothers* Muir
describes how he looked back in a dream and watched his dead
brothers playing and racing about the green as he had seen them
fifty years ago:

> I thought, how could I be so dull,
> Twenty thousand days ago,
> Not to see they were beautiful?
> I asked them, Were you really so
> As you are now, that other day?
> And the dream was soon away.
>
> For then we played for victory
> And not to make each other glad.

> A darkness covered every head,
> Frowns twisted the original face,
> And through that mask we could not see
> The beauty and the buried grace.

Muir also discovered that:

> Packed in my skin from head to toe
> Is one I know and do not know . . .
> His name's Indifference.
> Nothing offending he is all offence;
> Can stare at beauty's bosom coldly
> And at Christ's crucifixion boldly.[4]

In his autobiography Muir describes the effects of his being analysed. "My new self-knowledge had to burst through the resistance I put up, making great breaches and gashes in it, while I desperately tried to close them up again to preserve intact my old flattering image of myself. While my conscious mind was putting up this fight, my unconscious like a treacherous spy was enthusiastically working for the analyst . . . At last by painful stages I reached a state which resembled conviction of sin, though formulated in different terms. I realised the elementary fact that everyone, like myself, was troubled by sensual desires and thoughts, by unacknowledged failures and frustrations causing self-hatred and hatred of others, by dead memories of shame and grief which had been shovelled underground long since because they could not be borne. I saw that my lot was the human lot, that when I faced my own unvarnished likeness I was one among all men and women, all of whom had the same desires and thoughts, the same failures and frustrations, the same unacknowledged hatred of themselves and others, the same hidden shames and griefs, and that if they confronted these things they could win a certain liberation from them. It was really a conviction of sin, but even more a realisation of original sin." In a poem called *Comfort in Self Despite* Muir described how this greater self-knowledge leads to greater compassion and to the recovery of paradise.

Muir came to terms with his experience of evil in conclusions beyond the clear horrifying inconclusive vision of it in *The Combat*. The loss of paradise and the journey in the labyrinth of the world 'where nothing now can separate the corn and tares compactly grown' leads to human bewilderment and confusion, but not to final despair. Good—greater good is brought out of evil. 'Sin is necessary.'[5] Evil though strong and everywhere visible, is extremely vulnerable and as a product of time is not immortal. Out of it, greater good can come. A good man in hell would 'sow among the damned doubts of damnation' since 'one doubt of evil would bring down such a grace, open such a gate, all Eden would enter in'.

There is, it seems, a kind of unreality about evil: since Love is master in the sense that it will triumph in the end, and even now paradise is frequently regained and the kingdom visibly comes, penetrating time, and since it is clear that only the turn of a screw in the human brain could change seconds into years or a millennium into an hour, there is little hope of discerning Truth solely within the cage of human experience; that is, within the Story and without the Fable. "Life is a paradise," said Father Zossimer, "and we are all in paradise, only we do not wish to admit it."

Muir's poetic imagination is mainly concerned with personal life: he is a poet of the human condition. At least from his published writings there is nothing to suggest that he was astronomically or microscopically minded. He was concerned with planetary matters and not, as David Gascoyne for example was, with the apparent insignificance of life in terms of the cosmos—'a little mould on a grain of dust'. "The life of the human race," said Bernard Shaw, "is a brief and discreditable episode in the history of one of the meanest of planets." "Life," said Sir James Jeans, "may be a disease which attacks planets in their decay." Uncomplimentary comments of this kind are common enough. Muir was more concerned with the particularities of human suffering and happiness than with such vast conjectures. For him the aspirations of human beings are parts of the normal human endowment and are self-authenticating. Like some other parts of the universe they are still as 'clean as on the starting day'.

In the introduction to her collected poems, Kathleen Raine has written: "It was David Gascoyne who said to me that nature remains always in the Year One ... The ever-recurring forms of nature mirror eternal reality, the never-recurring productions of human history reflect only fallen man." Unlike Kathleen Raine who omitted all her poems which 'belong to the transient and not to the imaginative order', Muir's creative imagination was fired by the never-recurring events of human history. "Nature," he had said, "is always new and has no background; it is society that is old." A human being cannot abstract himself from society and live like an animal purely in the moment. He is a debtor to the past and is bound to it.

Time

Muir in later life believed firmly in immortality. "If man is an animal by direct descent I can see human life only as a nightmare populated by animals wearing top hats and kid gloves." In 1919 he had cast off, under the influence of Nietzsche, all belief in any other life than the life we live here and now as an imputation on the purity of immediate experience, which "I had intellectually convinced myself was guiltless and beyond good and evil". In the same year, he was sitting opposite a man in a tramcar in Glasgow and the words came into his mind, 'That is an animal.' He looked round the tram at the other occupants, and saw that they were all animals, "some of them good, some evil, some charming, some sad, some happy, some sick, some well ... and I realised that in all Glasgow, in all Scotland, in all the world, there was nothing but millions of such creatures all living an animal life and moving towards an animal death as towards a great slaughter house ..." The vision was so terrifying that he dismissed it immediately. "As I sat in that tramcar in Glasgow I was in an unhistorical world; I was outside time without being in eternity; in the small sensual momentary world of a beast." "But," says Muir writing many years later, "I believe that man has a soul and that it is immortal ... My belief in immortality so far as I can define its origin, and that is not far, seems to be connected with the same impulse which urges me to know myself." He says that the attempt at self-knowledge means that he will attend and listen to a class of experience which a disbeliever in immortality ignores or dismisses as irrelevant to temporal life. "These experiences come when I am least aware of myself as a personality moulded by my will and Time, in moments of contemplation when I am unconscious of my body, or indeed that I have a body with separate members, in moments of grief or prostration, in happy hours with friends, and, because self forgetfulness is most complete then, in dreams and daydreams in that floating half discarnate state which precedes and follows sleep. In these hours there seems to be knowledge of my real self and simultaneously knowledge of immortality. Sleep tells us things about ourselves which we could not discover otherwise."

In a diary in which he admits to have been writing when he was more unhappy than he had been at any time since the time of his obscure fears and the course of psycho-analysis which dispelled them, he writes as sadly as at the time of his vision of the animals in the tramcar at Glasgow: "We all come out of a hole and go back into a hole. Leave hiding and go back into hiding. The distance between is disguise." Later: "I can see men and women as really human only when I see them as immortal souls. Otherwise they are unnatural, self-evidently not what they are by nature; they do not exist in their own world.'

It was at this time (February 1939) that he saw some schoolboys playing marbles; "the old game had come round again at its own time, known only to children, and it seemed a little rehearsal for a resurrection promising a timeless renewal of life. That night I wrote in my diary: Last night going to bed alone I suddenly found myself (I was taking off my waistcoat) reciting the Lord's Prayer in a loud emphatic voice—a thing I had not done for many years—with deep urgency and profound disturbed emotion. While I went on I grew more composed; as if it had been empty and craving and were being replenished, my soul grew still; every word had a strange fullness of meaning which astonished and delighted me . . . Now I realised that quite without my knowing it, I was a Christian, no matter how bad a one . . . I did not turn to any church . . . I had no conception of the splendours of Christendom; I remained quite unaware of them until some years later I was sent by the British Council to Italy." It was then that he saw the visible signs of the Incarnation 'not only in churches but on the walls of houses, at crossroads in the suburbs, in wayside shrines in the parks and in private rooms'. All this seemed, after his upbringing in the United Presbyterian Church in Orkney, 'to be right, just as it was right that my Italian friends should step out frankly into life'.

"Life," said William Empson, "involves maintaining oneself between contradictions which cannot be solved by analysis." This is not a tragic predicament, though it is an inevitable one. But the greater the awareness of the tensions the greater also the zest for living and the acceptance of the conditions of life as the proper scene for the development and eventual fruition of the human person. In a poem called *The Bird*, Muir watches a bird 'walking upon the air, like a schoolboy running and loitering, leaping and springing, pensively pausing, suddenly changing your mind, to turn at last on the heel of a wing-tip' and he asks where could be found 'a floor so perfect, so firm and so fair' for this 'so delicate walking and airy winging'. The last three lines of the poem ask the same question of the human being born into the world, all in the making.

> The wide-winged soul itself can ask no more
> Than such a pure, resilient and endless floor
> For its strong-pinioned plunging and soaring and upward
>   and upward springing.

This poem of gratitude and appreciation of the conditions of life in general corresponds to another of Muir's recurring ideas about his own life in particular. The way seems lost, no track or trace visible of 'the road, the errand, the prize, the part to play' that his forebears promised so fondly when he set out upon 'the famous way'.

> Then suddenly again I watch the old
> Worn saga write across my years and find,
> Scene after scene, the tale my fathers told
> But I in the middle blind, as Homer blind,

> Dark on the highway, groping in the light,
> Threading my dazzling way within my night.[6]

There is an even more explicit joyful acceptance of life in a poem called *The Birthday*. Here the whole is seen in terms of the original paradisial certainties, proving themselves to have been true in spite of all the empirical deviations imposed by time—'a footstep more, and his unblinded eyes saw far and near the fields of Paradise'. Experience is transfigured and its meaning becomes dazzlingly clear. The rags and tatters suddenly change into the garments of royalty as the unwilling prodigal is called and led by the hand back to his true home.

Transfiguration and the Labyrinth

The image of human life as a journey, a pilgrimage on a long road, is a common one. Muir uses it constantly. But the road is often a labyrinth and the way is frequently lost. The direction is ambiguous.

> Through countless wanderings,
> Hastenings, lingerings,
> From far I come,
> And pass from place to place
> In a sleep-wandering pace
> To seek my home.

In the same poem, *The Journey Back*, he sees himself in many lives:

> I must in other lives with many a leap
> Blindfold, must lodge in dark and narrow skulls
> With a few thoughts that pad from wall to wall
> And never get out . . .
>
> In all these lives I have lodged, and each a prison . . .
> But there's no end, and I could break my journey
> Now, here, without a loss, but that some day
> I know I shall find a man who has done good
> His long lifelong and is

Image of man from whom all have diverged.
The rest is hearsay. So I hie me back
To my sole starting point, my random self
That in these rags and tatters clothes the soul.

This quiet reflective and moving poem is a good example of Muir's sense of unity with all human beings in their common predicament of living in an aimless and inexplicable world, but he has retained his certainty, based on his childhood experiences that the Christian rumour is true, and that the Fable once it is known does make sense of the Story.

There is constantly in his poems this belief that paradise and undiscerned providence is always just behind the scenes, and will in the end be seen to bring strength out of weakness and make sense of the nonsense, bring truth out of the error and greater goodness out of the evil. This transmuting and transfiguring process—an essentially Christian idea—gives meaning to 'Time's long ruin' and restores the lost confidence and makes clear the glorious Fable all the time lively in the follies of the Story. One of his finest poems, *The Transfiguration*, describes how he and his companion experienced this transmuting, and saw the surrounding scenery as on 'the starting day' when 'earth and light and water entering there, gave back to us the clear unfallen world'.

A. N. Whitehead said that religion must make clear to popular understanding 'some eternal greatness incarnate in the passage of temporal Fact'. Many men have had experience of happiness and experience of misery of great intensity and have made nothing of them. Muir had both and has recorded them in his remarkable autobiography and in his poems. Both of these great books tell how, for one man, the temporal facts of his life became the vehicle of some eternal greatness. His autobiography ends: 'As I look back on the part of the mystery which is my own life, my own Fable, what I am aware of is that we receive more than we can give; we receive it from the past, on which we draw with every breath, but also—and this is a point of Faith—from the source of the mystery itself, by the means which religious people call Grace."

CHAPTER 4 NOTES

1. cf. note 5.
2. *A Birthday*.
3. *The Road*.
4. *Variations on a Time Theme IX*.
5. cf. Julian of Norwich, *Revelations of Divine Love*, ch. 27, Penguin Classics. The twelve following chapters in this remarkable book are an exposition of this idea. The Methuen edition has an excellent Introduction by Grace Warrack. cf. also *Evil and the God of Love* by John Hick, Macmillan, 1966, p. 374 ff.
6. *Too Much*.

5 MAN: HIS NATURE, PREDICAMENT AND HOPE

(1) The Old Testament

Man is formed of matter.[1] His every thought, feeling, action, his most transcendental conceptions, have their origin in, and are made possible by, the same basic particles as those from which the whole cosmos is built.

It is through the body, therefore, that man has to live.[2] His experiences are always physical experiences, even though they may be evoked by either physical or non-physical occasions—things, places, people, psychic events, mental concepts. Thus, happiness may come from wealth and success, from loving and being loved, from intellectual achievement, from moral or religious exaltation, but it is manifested in a state of physical well-being. Misery, likewise, is a clinically observable state. When a man is afraid, there is pain in his belly and his bowels, his face goes pale, his joints tremble; when he is in the depths of despair, he feels it to the marrow of his bones, and his heart-beat becomes feeble and irregular; when greed or lust are frustrated, he falls ill or loses all appetite and energy. The physical balance of a sensitive person may be more disabled by a cruel word than someone else's by a cruel blow. Man's capacity to work and to accomplish is similarly vulnerable; he swings between an intense vitality which dares and performs incredible things and a reduced condition which cannot attempt or even desire anything, and which sees no point in going on. And because our existence is physical or it is nothing, we can even aptly and accurately describe the quality of our life—'good and full', 'wretched and futile'—by marking it on a scale of which the zero is clinical death. To say that we feel 'half-dead' is no wild or forced use of words.

By the same token, when death does come, the person dissolves and ceases.[3] Thereafter he can affect no one, for he has neither the power nor the means to act. He goes out into darkness and silence, and only his memory, kept alive in his people, or the continuance of his sons, or the solid achievements of his mind and strength, or even, it may be, his relics, extend what once he was.

But the paradox of man's being[4] is that, though he is thus physical through and through, he is also something much more—a non-physical reality, a person. This truth is bound up with his self-awareness, which is of such a kind that he can address himself as 'thou', and speak of his own personhood as if it were another being, someone whom he can judge, exhort, or comfort. This personhood is a different kind of fact from the fact of his body; indeed, it is the determinative, classifying fact about him, so that it is only right to speak of even a deceased human being as a 'dead person', and not just as a physical object. Accordingly, to treat a dead man or woman as so much debris is a mark of inhumanity, and to be so treated is a just fate for the worst of mankind.

This is one reason why the human thread, while woven firmly into the rich tapestry of existence, is yet different in kind[5] from the rest of the fabric. Looked at as an organic whole rather than analytically, man has no peer outside his own species, and for this he is indebted primarily to his mental and psychic life. Many animals are stronger than he; he falls an easy victim to disease or accident. His expectation of life is miserably short, especially for a being of such potential. But despite all these limitations he has the capacity to dominate the world, and to subdue almost everything in it to his will. This domination is not merely a possibility to him, but a necessity, a law of his being; from one standpoint, it is what he is for. And all this is made feasible by his powers of reason and understanding. He is the being who gives names to things, and so imposes pattern and order; who observes similarities and relationships. It is this quality of wisdom which makes possible all other achievements.

Nevertheless, even though he may be lord of the world, man is not lord of everything.[6] The nature of his ultimate master is made clear to him by the universal doom of mortality—time is the enemy who always wins, eternity the kingdom he can never enter. This is all the more bitter to him because of the mental superiority which enables him at least to conceive of eternity. But if he is barred from eternity, who does live there? If it is not empty, then the one whose home it is must enjoy absolute and ultimate power, and from him all secondary authorities must derive.

Man in general has been only too ready to believe that there are any number of such beings.[7] He has imagined a whole invisible world of superhuman personalities interlocking with the visible order, and exerting emphatic influences upon it. He has fancied that these influences operated through media in the natural world—heavenly bodies, trees, stones, animals, and so forth—or that the beings responsible for them could be induced to enter sacred artefacts or dwell in consecrated buildings. These convictions appear to be compulsive for the majority of the human race, but they are the figments of a besotted imagination, which a few moments' rational thought would expose for the nonsense they are. Nevertheless, men go on treating these beings in whom they believe, with respect, as if they did exist, and did in fact have the will and power to answer human requests; and men commit any atrocity to propitiate them, quite undeterred by the fact that no results ever accrue to justify either the respect or the requests. These gods and demons have the mindless, cyclic character of the processes of nature which they are wrongly supposed to control; and so it is hardly surprising that their worshippers can think of nothing better to do in their honour than to allow the processes of nature within themselves mindless and impersonal expression. Or, if the course of events seems haphazard, men will invest even the random with the dignity of personality, and degrade themselves by worshipping fate and destiny. Or again, they seek access to the supernatural with the help of charlatans who claim special powers, such as foreseeing the future from the heavenly bodies, or communing with the dead.

But there is only One who inhabits eternity.[8] He is not a prisoner of the world; he is distinct from it, and presides over it. In himself he is unknowable, because he cannot be directly observed, nor is there anything in the cosmos with which he can properly be compared. Not even miraculous man is a true index of that wisdom, that power.

The world, therefore, does not have supreme value, but it has real value of its own.[9] It functions in accordance with its own regularities; it generates life from within itself. All its living creatures each obey, mysteriously but perfectly, the law of their being.

This world is not a closed system.[10] Its whole nature is determined not by itself but by the Lord of eternity; even its unshakeable stability comes from him, and could equally easily be taken away by him. Irresistible though the forces of nature may seem, they are as nothing to his power, which is supremely shown in the effortlessness of his creative act. Furthermore, this creating is no blind or random process; it is the expression of a concept and a plan, and may therefore be compared to the utterance of a word or a command —an utterance which is sufficient, without any further action, to achieve its ends, and to maintain them at all times.

Likewise, man himself is not a closed system.[11] His personality can be invaded by realities distinct from the contents of his own psyche. This is seen when men suddenly behave in ways quite alien both to their own character hitherto, and to the general conventions of human beings. But men may also be directed, and their powers intensified, by outside influences; and supremely by that incomparable power which comes from the Lord of eternity. For that Lord is not concerned merely to uphold cosmic order; he also has a dynamic purpose of creative change, seeking to develop a new good within the universe. In this purpose man and his history play a vital part; for the grand design behind existence is nothing less than a vast mesh of mutual dependences and responsibilities.

This is seen first of all in the relation between man and the world.[12] Man is utterly dependent on the world, in the sense that if the resources of nature are hard to come by, he has a struggle to survive, and if they are denied altogether he perishes. Moreover, everything he does has to be done within the framework of fact which was laid down by the decisive primal events unimaginable ages before the human race emerged. In every practical activity there is a wise course, which submits to the givenness of the world, and an unwise course which ignores it. But nature also needs man. It is dependent upon him to realise the potential of good present in the natural order; and this means that men have been given their power to dominate the world not simply, or even primarily, that they may enjoy it, but as a responsibility to care for it, and to enable it to fulfil its proper destiny.

The same mutual dependence and responsibility marks the relations between human beings.[13] Men are inextricably involved with one another; nor do they relate merely as pairs of isolated individuals to have a relationship with someone is to incur concern and obligation in some appropriate degree for all the other people who are bound to them.

Highest among all human relationships is that of man and wife.[14] Where it exists, it must take precedence over every other. Indeed, when it is necessary to determine the course of a person's life by an absolute obligation to the community at large or to a transcendent cause, marriage has to be avoided altogether, since if it were not it would inevitably and properly create conflict. The essence of the marriage relationship, however, does not lie in the sexual union alone, which is something that may have to be renounced when higher duties are at stake. The heart of it is the special degree of mutual commitment and knowledge which it entails; and that is why the quality of a marriage is dependent upon the qualities of character of the partners. So profound and satisfying can this relationship be that it can even compensate for the lack of children, and it is the natural consolation for the loss of a parent in death. When a man has found the right partner, almost any effort or sacrifice is worthwhile to win her; and to deny the marriage bond the reverence which is its due is the cruellest sacrifice that can be demanded of anyone.

Such an evaluation of marriage is impossible without a belief in the fundamental equality of the sexes.[15] Whatever the economic or social conventions of a particular generation or society, woman is a man's only true compeer; no other being in this world supplies the needs of his whole person as she does, nor does any being other than himself supply hers. Women may be as important as men in the community; they may hold the highest positions of power; their advice in public affairs, even in war, is as good as any man's; they can be as ruthless and violent; they can be wealthy property-owners, expert employers and business people; and they have equal rights in the eyes of the Eternal.

Marriage leads the individual out into an ever-increasing network of dependences and responsibilities, which is the proper sphere of his life. Brought up in the family,[16] the greatest happiness is to have a family of one's own, where parents have their duties to their children, and children to their parents. But one's own household is only part of the new involvement. A brother's family may be as much a man's care as his own; and then there is concern for the family to which one is linked by marriage, for parents-in-law as well as parents. Duty to one's kin is of such importance that to enable it to be fulfilled the state is justified in remitting the sentence on a convicted murderer. Finally, respect for the heads of families extends into respect for all the aged; where there is no proper reverence for those who have endured and achieved, values have become radically distorted.

For, after all, the natural way of thinking about the community is as the family writ large.[17] This is, in any case, a simple fact; and it is for the good of human life that people should not be allowed to forget it. Every man's bereaved is my bereaved, every man's poor my poor. Even an unquestioned legal right cannot justify me in depriving another man of the necessities of existence; economic principles alone must not be allowed to dictate my dealings with men in general any more than with my own family, nor must my personal likes or dislikes. Every man (even the rich!) has equal rights before the law. Retribution may not be left to the vindictiveness of the individual; vendetta, or the escalation of revenge, is utterly impermissible. Wealth or social status are ultimately of no significance whatever. When the community is set over against the Eternal, and its members are considered in the light of the universal human condition, all are of equal intrinsic value.

The same holds good for the larger association of the state.[18] The relation of rulers to ruled, and of any leader or commander to his fellow men, is quasi-parental. Furthermore, just as each member of a family has a right to a share in the resources of the family, whether or not he or she is still productive and useful, so each member of the nation has an irreducible claim to a stake in the real wealth of the nation, and this claim must be respected even against the run of commercial development. This is not a right of property. The natural resources on which a state is utterly dependent are not the creation of the state; they were there before the state came into existence, they are part of the givenness of its condition. Hence they belong not to the state itself, nor to any individual, but to the Eternal. And it is under the Eternal that each human being, in order to live out his natural destiny, must, wherever he can handle it have the trusteeship of some part of that environment vested in himself, and where he cannot, must make what contribution is in him, and benefit by the trusteeship of others. 'From each according to his ability; to each according to his need'—but the centralisation of trusteeship in the hands of government leads only to the dehumanisation of the individual man.

And what is true of the state is true also of the whole human race[19]—it is one gigantic family, and behaviour between nations, rulers, and individual members of different nations, ought to conform to this pattern. There are rules and conventions of conduct which one human being, of whatever race, ought to follow in dealing with a fellow man, and which he has a right to expect will be observed towards himself. Likewise, the deeper personal relation of freely chosen friendship brings with it obligations akin to those of family life.

And the universe—what of that? This final sum of the givenness of things dwarfs man into insignificance, and was certainly not planned merely to serve his good. Many of its facts may be actively hostile to him; but this does not make them evil, for they have as much right to be themselves as he. Man comes late on the cosmic scene; the vastly greater part of it has no relevance to him at all, even within his own planet. But just as within a human family the members each have a different and yet valid worth, so it is with the universe and all its elements in their relationship with one another. The pattern is still essentially a family pattern; and every thing that is not the Eternal can call that Eternal 'Father'.

Obedience to the facts of man's nature and situation would certainly call for life of some such quality as this; but it is clear enough that this ideal is not realised. The failures are of two kinds. On the one hand, the demands of the human condition are not met; on the other, that condition itself is resented. What should have been man's world has become his predicament.

The symptoms of this double failure are many[20] and various. Man does not come near to realising his own physical potential; his failure to live obediently within the human condition, to meet its demands, deprives him of his proper scope of time. His relationship with other living things is too often one of terror and death. He deals ill with the inanimate world; he is at war with the earth, and it denies him his livelihood or yields it only to his toil and tears.

Another crop of symptoms, and an abundant one, is found in the relations of human beings to one another.[21] Every requirement which has been mentioned as arising from the interplay of the family pattern of human life with the givenness of the world and of man's condition is regularly violated. The husband tyrannises over his wife as an inferior, and the wife perverts her husband. Brother murders brother—indeed, all murder is the murder of a brother. The son will slander his father, and conspire to kill him. One brother will defraud another of his natural rights; and the wise man will trust his friend rather than his relations any day. In the larger family of the community, the worker is denied the just rewards of his work; men take advantage of the handicapped. Any means to a quick profit is considered justified. Perjury is used to secure the condemnation of an innocent fellow citizen at law, even to the point of engineering his execution. In the building up of property and commercial empires thousands are deprived of their rightful share in the trusteeship of the world's resources, and are pauperised, reduced to the proletariat, or sold into slavery. In relations between states some nations abandon all decency or human feeling and break every convention. In every sphere truth, loyalty, positive well-doing, respect for personhood, self-discipline, are disregarded.

But in addition to all the miseries which he brings upon himself by his failure to meet the demands of the human condition man labours under yet another deep and poignant agony—the sense of the futility of his own existence.[22] This sense of futility can, and in practice often does, break the will to act responsibly. This is not just a matter of the absence of any relation between virtue and happiness (though this discourages many)—it is a feeling that the discrepancy between man's ability to imagine permanence and the actual transience to which he is condemned is an injustice. Why should he exert himself to create what is beautiful, do what is good, discover what is true, when none of it lasts? Why should he put himself out to care for others, when love comes to a more wretched end than cruelty? It is not a question of reward; it is that the destiny of what is good *ought* to be better than that of evil. It ought in fact to be eternal; but, so far as anyone can tell, it is not. If so, then values can have no more than a purely utilitarian function, and should be adjusted to be as practical as possible, in other words, to make the best of the fact of transience. And to one who feels this way a personal and vivid awareness of the Eternal brings no solace; it merely annihilates the spirit, robbing a man even of the illusion of self-respect.

And yet it is possible to imagine something better,[23] an attitude of mind and heart in which the human condition is accepted without resentment, where life is lived to the full, and death is accepted as ripeness, as the just and tranquil goal; where a man's personality is a unified thing, consistently and freely willing what is good, and playing its appropriate part towards each member of the human family, important or unimportant. And if this can be conceived, why can it not be actualized? What is—what was—the reason?

There are in fact two reasons. The first is the inescapable conflict within man[24] between the two fundamental forces of his being, forces utterly necessary to him and yet mutually antagonistic. On the one hand he must assert himself, express himself, impose his own pattern on his world, control, dominate. This, as we saw, is a law of his existence; it is this which makes it possible for him to be an artist or craftsman, a poet or musician, a ruler or counsellor, to amass wealth and to build, to raise children. On the other hand, he is also a co-operator, social, ready to compromise, to sacrifice himself, seeking affection and approval. His desire is to live in peace; he detests war. His loneliness cries out for companionship. And this too is integral to him, part of the way he is made. It leads him to mercy and compassion, to gentleness, humility, and wisdom. But these forces cannot be relied upon to spend themselves only in those ways that accord with the true needs of the human condition. The first may equally lead to murder, war, robbery, violence, revenge, lust, tyranny, and genocide. Not merely individuals, but communities and states can and do give themselves up to unbridled self-assertion. The second may produce cowardice and treachery, falsehood, and refusal to acknowledge unpleasant reality. And when imbalance or misapplication of these forces within each individual interacts with similar distortion and malfunctioning in everyone else, the doom of chaos falls on the whole race.

The second and complementary reason is the limitation of man's capacities.[25] He can know what is good and what is bad, pleasant and unpleasant; he can know other people, and himself. But only to a certain extent. His own heart and the hearts of his fellows are ultimately a mystery to him; the final results and repercussions of his actions are hidden from him. The nature of the world he only very partially understands. He can do but only so much; he can care for others, but only ineffectually.

When these two facts, the inner conflict and the limitation of capacity, are taken together, then it becomes clear that man is fated either to live imperfectly or not to live at all.[26] Decision is possible to him, because he has reasons, values, affections by which to plot his course; he must decide, because if he does not satisfy his inner forces he withers away. But he can never get his decision right. He is under a necessity of error.

In one sense, then, man's failure is only a function of his frailty and finitude. To this at most a very reduced culpability attaches, and perhaps none at all. But this is not all there is to be said. In the first place, man refuses to recognise his limitations.[27] Because he can take decisions, he concludes that he can take right decisions — 'right' not in the perfectly reasonable sense of the 'best he can do', but right 'absolutely'. Because he is aware of good and evil and can distinguish roughly between their more obvious instances, he believes that he knows and understands good and evil in their essence and everywhere. Man's characteristic utterance is not, 'I will do this even though I know it to be wrong', but, 'I will do this because I am satisfied that it is right, at any rate in this case'; and this applies whether his purposes are ones of life or of death. But good and evil are part of the givenness of the totality of things, which is both before and greater than Man, and which cannot be known except to the Eternal. To act as if this were not so is to regard oneself, or mankind at large, as the Eternal — and this, whether it calls itself religion or humanism, is nonsense, and an arrogance which in the end the nature of things inevitably shows up for nonsense. What, therefore, might have been innocent and tolerable shortcoming, now becomes lunatic pride.

Secondly, man tries to avoid taking responsibility.[28] But he cannot be man unless he will take it. His awareness of himself as a self in relation to other selves finds expression in language in the word 'ought'. If he refuses to submit to the 'ought', whatever its content, or even to acknowledge its existence, he denies his own nature. Even in face of the Eternal, man must stand up and take responsibility for what he is; and to pass the blame elsewhere is to degrade oneself. It may objectively be true that other people and circumstances are largely, even overwhelmingly the cause of our character and behaviour; but the only way forward to genuine human stature is to take responsibility for what we are, whether this is factually a fair and accurate description of the situation or no. Man needs to be confronted by the 'You shall' and the 'You shall not' which give him dignity. To refuse them is death; to accept them is the way through to life.

The predicament of man therefore has three aspects. First, there is his inability to meet the demands of his condition, because of internal conflict which he cannot avoid, and of limits to his capacity which he cannot transcend. Secondly, there is his inability to accept the terms of his condition, because he is aware of the possibility of something more, something for which he feels himself fitted by the very nature of personal life. Thirdly, the living of this life, with its conflicts and limitations, its frustration and resentment, means inevitable failure in respect of that sense of obligation which is inseparable from his awareness of himself in relation to other selves — and this failure means a sense of guilt.[29] And because this sense of guilt arises from a failure to meet the demands of that givenness of things which is rooted in primal and decisive events outside the reach of his knowledge, it is not an experience simply of guilt towards his fellow beings on earth, but in the last analysis of guilt against the Eternal.

Man's need is to be delivered from this predicament in all its aspects, and his hope is that this need will somehow be met. This is in truth the only hope relevant to the human condition; any other must be a palliative or an anodyne. But the predicament and the need are themselves the work of the Eternal, because it is with the givenness of things that man is at war; and therefore it is the Eternal alone who can in the end reconcile man to his condition, and give him fulfilment of his hope. The question is: How might this be done?

First, there is the dual problem of inner conflict and limited capacity.[30] The conflict may be expressed in another way by seeing it as the question of the individual and the group: how to achieve simultaneously the incompatible fulfilments of imposing oneself on one's environment, including other people, and of subordinating oneself to them in co-operation and sacrifice. So long as the human situation is understood as a confrontation of independent selves, clearly there can be no resolution of the problem. At the very least what is needed is a vision of life as a partnership of selves in a shared purpose. But it will not do for this purpose to be simply the goal envisaged by *one* self and accepted by others; on this basis the conflict of self-assertion and co-operation is not resolved but ignored. The purpose must be that set by the givenness of the human condition, and recognised by all for what it is—in other words, a purpose in conformity with the will of the Eternal. Man's need, therefore, is to feel that he himself and those with whom he is in relationship are equal partners in the service of the Eternal specified by each situation.

But this at once raises the other half of the dual problem: how is man, with his limited capacities, to discern precisely what is the good,[31] the purpose of the Eternal in each fragmentary situation? If man is in fact an open, not a closed system, then he is susceptible to guidance and stimulation from outside himself. Can he hope that such guidance will be given him, and if so, in what form? Can he be filled with an inspiration which will enable him to transcend the slowness and narrow scope of his spirit without at the same time taking away his freedom? Can he be given an intuition which will speak the truth as and when required? Can he develop a spontaneity of heart which will of its own motion conform both to the purposes of existence and to the love of other beings? Is it possible that his limitations in the systematic intellectual study of the world might be overcome, and he learn to see it and interpret it with the same mind and values as those of the Eternal from whom the primal decisions come? Can he, in fact, have the Eternal within himself and within all other men, so that they are truly one at the deepest level, and the problems of the self *vis-à-vis* the group are resolved?

Secondly, there is man's need to be rescued from his sense of futility[32] and injustice. This sense is not unwarrantable presumption on man's part. To be able to conceive of eternity and to be denied it; to be able to create what is worthy to endure, and to know it must pass; this is in truth a futility and a frustration. It might be thought that what men needed in this predicament was an assurance of life, everlasting life beyond death. But if realism about death, which means in fact about the nature of man, is to be retained, how can such an assurance be given? The two things are incompatible. Nor, in these circumstances, would life beyond death really draw the sting of death. What is the purpose of annihilation, if it is to be repaired afterwards? Is it to test those who endure to the end, thus making the restored life a kind of reward for irrational virtue? And if it is, then virtue may become more rational, but does it not cease to be virtue? Man's need is primarily for something which will take the futility from *this* life. Not until this is done can life beyond death be acceptable as morally and rationally coherent with this one; but when it is done, then man ceases to worry whether there is to be a life beyond or not—and so it becomes possible to give him one without the risk of corrupting him in so doing. Man's need and hope, therefore, is for a living sense of partnership with the Eternal, that the Eternal should, as it were, wear a human face, and admit man into his friendship here and now; and that from this partnership man should derive a positive value which crowds out the futility felt by him in his isolation, replacing it with deep and abiding satisfaction.

Thirdly, man needs to be delivered from guilt.[33] Again, at first sight it might seem that there was a simple answer—forgiveness. But forgiveness does not deal with guilt at all; it deals with personal relationship. It says that the facts of the past, and the guilt which they occasioned, are not to count; they are not to be allowed to affect present conduct. Forgiveness cries, 'Let us stop, and start again with a clean sheet.' But when this has been said, the forgiven party is still the guilty party; remorse, and the evil consequences of his fault remain. It is this which leads men to seek to expiate their wrongdoing, to outweigh their unjustified self-pleasing with self-torment, sometimes extreme. But how can the past be changed? It is just conceivable that over the future one might exercise some control, but the past is written for ever. Is there really nothing to be done save to accept it? Acceptance there must be, acceptance of oneself and one's life and of the life of the whole race; but beyond acceptance is there no unmerited hope? Cannot the Eternal change evil into good?

Let us suppose that somewhere, some time, some member of the human family did succeed in living a life in accordance with the givenness of the human condition, in line with the will of the Eternal.[34] If a man did live such a life, it would of course be one in which he himself incurred no guilt with regard to his fellows; but even more it would be one in which they co-operated with him in the purpose of the Eternal, even though they were blind to that purpose and to him as its instrument. Such blindness, such evil intentions, would mean his suffering, as he took them upon himself, and brought them into co-operation with the Eternal. They might deny him any seeming success or even successors. But his awareness of goodness and truth, and his submission to them, would in the end prevail, even beyond his own annihilation. For when men recognised what he had done, they would see that from then onwards the human family could indeed hold up its head in pride, since in one of its members, at least, it had achieved the purpose of its existence. And to continue the task of this one man's life would be a sufficient role for all men and all time thereafter. And if—if—this human life were the work of the Eternal himself, then indeed man could feel himself reconciled to his condition, and joyful in the givenness of things.

Such a release from his predicament would free man,[35] and enable him to take on his right role in the cosmos, working for all those needs of his fellow-beings which they could not attain for themselves or by themselves. A world of abundance and peace, with no starving millions; a world of order among men, where the rulers were the blessed of the ruled, and among all creatures; a world of fullness of life and years and health, of knowledge and love. A world in fact where everything gave glory to the Eternal in manifesting the wisdom and generosity of his design, a world which he could properly and fittingly remake in order to incorporate it into his eternity, to destroy death, and to preserve for ever the family structure—with all its members—of which he is the only true Father.

CHAPTER 5 NOTES

It would be a mistake to assume that there was ever any Old Testament Jew who held all the views about man, put forward in this chapter, simultaneously. For one thing the books of the Old Testament cover a period roughly equal to that from the Norman Conquest to our own day, and even if change was slower than in modern times, change both in knowledge and understanding of man and his world there undoubtedly was. The 'Old Testament view of man', therefore, is in a sense a purely theoretical construct. Nevertheless, because Israel was an entity with immensely enduring traditional forms and ideas—a group which believed that it owed the whole structure of its life to a gift of God in the past—the gap between individuals and generations makes less difference than it does with us. There is a family likeness in the thinking of all the Old Testament writers; they are executing their own variations on a common theme of man. It is that theme which we have tried to outline. The documentation for it follows.

1. 'The Lord God formed man of dust from the ground'; 'You are dust, and to dust you shall return' (Gen. 2:7; 3:19; cf. Ps. 90:3, R.S.V.). In view of our modern preconceptions it ought to be stressed that the 'breath of life' which God breathed into man and into all the animals (Gen. 7:15, 22; Ps. 104:29) is not to be thought of as 'soul' or 'spirit', but as physical breath, air in motion.

2. For a splendid picture of the happiness that comes from wealth and status cf. Job 29; from love, Song of Solomon (also Prov. 15:17); from intellectual achievement, Prov. 3:13–18; from moral and religious exaltation, Ps. 73:26, 84:5, 16:11, 17:15. There is an abundance of passages in which the clinical effects of misery are described; the symptoms mentioned in the text will be found in the following and many other places: Isa. 13:8; Jer. 4:19 (correct translation, 'My bowels!'); Nahum 2:10; Ps. 22:14, 38:3; Isa. 13:7, 19:1; II Sam. 13:2; I Kings 21:4. For the savage effect of a cruel word cf. Prov. 17:10. The hero stories of Israel's early days, preserved in Joshua and Judges; the stories of Saul (I Sam. 11) and David (I Sam. 17) and of the early prophets (I Kings 18–19), and the very different record of such a man as Jeremiah (cf. esp. 11:21, 18:18, 20:1–2, 20:7–12, 26:7–24, 32:2–5,

36, 37:11–21, 43:1–7)—all show how deeply embedded in Israel's tradition was the sense of what one great man could achieve against impossible odds. By contrast, man at the end of his tether is classically portrayed in Job 3. The idea of life as a scale, with wretchedness close to the zero of actual death, is frequent; it is expressed in such phrases as 'to be brought down to Sheol', i.e., 'place of the departed': cf., e.g., Ps. 18:4–5, 22:15, 88:3–6, 15.

3. No one will ever put this better than the wise woman of Tekoa: 'We are like water spilt on the ground, which cannot be gathered up again' (II Sam. 14:14, R.S.V.). For the impotence of the dead cf. the taunting of the shades against the newly-slain king of Babylon, Isa. 14:9–11; for death as darkness, Ps. 88:12, and silence, Ps. 115:17. One way in which Abraham is to be immortalised is in the grateful memory of all mankind (Gen. 18:18); the childless Nehemiah writes his memoirs so that his services to Israel shall not be forgotten (Neh. 5:19, 13:31). Continuation in one's offspring is a general human ambition; its importance in Israel is illustrated by, e.g., Abraham's complaint to God, Gen. 15:1–6. Absalom, David's errant son, was, according to one tradition, childless, and built a monument to preserve his name for posterity (II Sam. 18:18). On the subject of relics, cf. the popular legend in II Kings 13:20–21, and the taking of Joseph's bones back to Canaan: Gen. 50:25; Exod. 13:19.

4. In the older English versions of the Old Testament the word 'soul' appears frequently, rendering the Hebrew word *nephesh*. In the majority of instances 'soul' should today be replaced by 'person', to avoid the suggestion of a 'ghost-in-the-machine', which is foreign to Hebrew thought. In the famous verse, Gen. 2:7, the modern version ('man became a living being', R.S.V.) conveys the meaning better. How *nephesh* can mean 'person' is well illustrated in Gen. 12:5, which refers to the slaves Abram and Lot had bought in Mesopotamia; cf. also Gen. 46:26–27. For a man addressing his own person cf. Ps. 42:5, 11, 43:5. The distinction between personhood and the body is unmistakably drawn in the language of Ps. 63:1, 73:26, where the pairs of terms are certainly not used simply to say 'I' twice. For the corpse as a 'dead person' cf. Num. 6:6, where R.S.V. 'body' is the equivalent of Heb. *nephesh* again. For the terrible fate of being denied respectful treatment after death cf., among many other passages, Ps. 79:2; Isa. 14:19–20; Eccl. 6:3.

5. The fact that man is at home in the pageant of the world is superbly

expressed in Ps. 104, which should be read as a whole (note the perfect
placing of v. 23). For his uniqueness, cf. Gen. 2:20. On strong animals,
Job 39:9–12, 19–25; I Sam. 17:37; Ps. 33:17; disease, Isa. 38:10–13;
I Kings 17:17; II Kings 4:18–37; on accident, II Kings 7:16–20.
On the shortness of human life, cf. Ps. 90:5–6, 10, 144:4. Man's capacity
to dominate the world is made a primal ordinance of the cosmos in
Gen. 1:28–29, 9:1–3; Ps. 8:5–9, and thus the very purpose of his
existence. For reason as a distinctive mark of Man cf. Ps. 32:9. In the
older of the two Creation stories Adam gives names to all the other
living creatures as they are formed by God (Gen. 2:19); this symbolises
both his sovereignty over them and his understanding of their true
nature. The whole 'wisdom' literature of Israel, notably Proverbs, is
based on the perception of similarities and relationships; for this ability
as the source of all others cf., e.g., Prov. 8:15–16.

6. Some references on the subject of mortality have already been
given, p. 110 above. In the present context cf. the elegiac beauty of
Job 14; also Ps. 102:23–24; Eccl. 8:8. 'He has put eternity into man's
mind', Eccl. 3:11, R.S.V.—some scholars wish to emend the text on the
grounds that the author could not have made such a profound remark,
or one so un-Hebrew; but, given his temperament, the Greek influences
upon him, and the Old Testament view of man, it fits in naturally
enough. For the description of God as 'the . . . One who inhabits
eternity', cf. Isa. 57:15, R.S.V. For Man's sovereignty as derived from
God, cf. Gen. 1:26, 28; Ps. 8:6–8.

7. The Old Testament is particularly scornful of the nature- and
culture-religions of its neighbours. On supernatural beings operating
through the heavenly bodies, cf. Deut. 4:19; Amos 5:26; trees and
stones, Jer. 3:9; animals (as media of demons), Isa. 13:21; Ps. 91:13.
For a biting attack on the sacred image industry cf. Isa. 44:9–20; for
the multitude of other references to images and sacred objects, cf.,
e.g., I Kings 12:28; Hos. 10:5, 13:2; Zech. 5:5–11; II Kings 23:4–14.
On the impossibility of God's dwelling in a temple, cf. Isa. 66:1, and the
pious sentiment put into Solomon's mouth at the dedication of his
temple in Jerusalem: I Kings 8:27. False religion universal: Ps. 96:5,
115:1–8, 135:15–18, 147:20; Deut. 4:19; repugnant to commonsense,
Isa. 44:20. On the atrocities connected with such religion cf. II Kings
3:27, 21:6; Ezek. 16:20; on its lack of results, Isa. 41:22–24, 45:20.
Men wrongly attribute control of Nature to these powers, Hos. 2:8. On
the orgiastic indulgences during the rites of the nature-religions, cf.,

e.g., Jer. 2:23–24, 3:23; on ecstatic self-mutilation: I Kings 18:28; Hos. 7:14. On the worship of Fate and Destiny, Isa. 65:11; astrology, Isa. 47:13; necromancy (or spiritualism?): Lev. 19:31; I Sam. 28:6–19; Isa. 8:19 cf. 57:9.

8. 'I am the first and I am the last; besides me there is no God,' Isa. 44:6, R.S.V.; cf. also Isa. 45:5, 6, 45:18. (Isa. 40–55 is a goldmine for affirmations of this truth.) Cf. also Deut. 6:4, the great daily prayer of Israel: 'The Lord our God, the Lord is One.' God presiding over the universe but not contained or limited by it: 'It is he who sits above the circle of the earth,' Isa. 40:22, R.S.V.—this, in Israelite cosmology, meant 'above the heavens', cf. Ps. 8:1, 113:6; also the ultimate statement of I Kings 8:27 R.S.V.: 'Heaven and the highest heaven cannot contain thee!' That God cannot be directly perceived with the senses is assumed, e.g., by stories like that of Elijah, I Kings 19:12–13, and by traditions such as those of the cloud and the fire, or the glory, which are signs to the Israelites in the wilderness that God is invisibly present with them; cf. Exod. 14:24, 16:10, 19:16–18; Num. 12:5–6; also an allusion to this, Isa. 4:5–6. A somewhat different concept is that God can be seen, but that Man either cannot endure the vision or is too sinful to be allowed it; cf. Exod. 32:30; Judges 13:22; Isa. 6:5; Ezek. 1:26–28; Job 42:5. The only way in which men are allowed, in a sense, to 'see' God is in the cult: Ex. 24:9–11; Ps. 27:8. For God's incomparability, Isa. 40:18; far outstripping even Man, Isa. 40:25–31.

9. 'And behold it was very good,' Gen. 1:31 R.S.V. The regular and reliable functioning of the universe aroused the wonder of a number of Old Testament writers: cf., esp. Gen. 8:22; Jer. 33:20; Ps. 104:9, 148:6. Gen. 1:20, 24 undoubtedly imply that earth and sea have been given the power of themselves to bring forth life. For the laws governing the behaviour of animals cf. Jer. 8:7, the migration of birds.

10. The stability of the cosmos as a gift of God, Ps. 75:3 R.S.V., 'When the earth totters, and all its inhabitants, it is I who keep steady its pillars.'; cf. Ps. 93:1; as something he may take away at will, cf. Gen. 7:11, which in terms of Ancient Near Eastern cosmology implies not just exceptional rain, but the breaking up of the whole structure of the universe. God mightier even than the greatest forces of nature, Ps. 93:4. The effortlessness of God's creative act could not be more vividly expressed than by the simple device of the writer of Gen. 1, 'And God said, "Let there be . . . ," and it was so', cf. vv. 3, 9, 11, 14–15, 24. The concept and plan behind creation are stressed in Prov. 8:22–31,

where 'wisdom' is God's 'architect' from the first; cf. Ps. 104:24. That even the regularities of the world are due to God's continuing will to maintain them is affirmed in passages such as Gen. 8:21–22, 9:12–16; the belief that he can, if he wishes, change or suspend them, is implicit in such a central story as that of the crossing of the Red Sea, Exod. 14–15. It is worth noting, however, how little the Old Testament asserts such intervention; for isolated examples cf. Josh. 10:12–14; Isa. 38:8.

11. The classic case of a man whose character undergoes a sudden and vicious deterioration is that of Saul, who from being a modest (I Sam. 10:21–24) and humane (I Sam. 15:9) man, became insanely jealous and cruel (I Sam. 18:10–11, 25, 20:33, 22:11–19). The Old Testament ascribes this to an 'evil spirit', where we might talk of the stresses of his position aggravated by the defection of Samuel (I Sam. 15:24–35); in either case external forces are recognised as to blame. For the intensification of powers by superhuman inspiration cf., e.g., Judges 14:19, 15:14–16; I Sam. 11:6 ff. (military valour); I Kings 18:46 (physical prowess); Exod. 35:30–36:1 (artistic skill and craftsmanship); Isa. 61:1–4 (religious insight); Ezra 7:27; and many other passages. God's purpose of creative change: Isa. 45:18, 46:9–10; new good, Isa. 43:19; use of history, II Sam. 17:14; I Kings 22:19–23; Isa. 10:5–19, 41:2–4; Hab. 1:5–11; Hag. 2:6–9; Esther 4:14.

12. Struggle for survival: an unending theme in the hard world of the Old Testament, cf., e.g., Gen. 42–45; I Kings 17–18; Joel 1; Hag. 1:6; Mal. 3:10–11. Primal events ages before man, Job 38:4–7 ('Where were you ... ?'). Wisdom in practical activity, cf., e.g., Isa. 28:23–29 (agriculture). On man's duty and responsibility for the world cf. Gen. 2:15 R.S.V., where Adam is put into paradise not just to enjoy it, but 'to till it and to keep it'; for a picture of what man might do for nature, cf. the famous picture of the lion lying down with the lamb in the reign of the true and faithful king, Isa. 11 and Elsa in 'Born Free'.

13. Mutual involvement in its full depth and intensity, Gen. 44:30; I Sam. 18:3; II Sam. 15:21, 18:33. Responsibility for those connected, II Sam. 9; Gen. 45:17–20.

14. Precedence over other relationships, Gen. 2:24; over duty to the community, Deut. 20:7. Vocational celibacy, Jer. 16:1–4. Renunciation of sexual relations in obedience to higher duty, II Sam. 11:11. Mutual commitment: a true marriage calls for loyalty, even when the partner is no longer young and attractive, Mal. 2:14–16. Mutual knowledge:

H

the verb 'to know' is used in Hebrew of the consummation of a marriage,
Gen. 4:1. Marriage dependent on the personal qualities of the partners:
Prov. 12:4, 18:22, 19:14, 25:24, 27:15–16, 31:10–31; Ruth 3:11.
Compensation for lack of children, I Sam. 1:8; for loss of a parent,
Gen. 24:67. Any effort worthwhile to win right partner, Gen. 29:20.
Cruellest sacrifice demanded of prophet Ezekiel was the command not to
mourn for his dead wife, Ezek. 24:15–24.

15. Woman is a man's only true compeer, Gen. 2:20–23. Women as
important as men in the community, Judges 4:4–5; holding supreme
power, II Kings 11:3; advice in public affairs, II Sam. 20:16–22, war,
Judg. 4:6–8. Women ruthless and violent, Judges 4:21, cf. 5:24–27;
I Kings 19:2, 21:7–15; II Kings 11:1. Women as wealthy property-
owners, II Kings 4:8; expert employers and business people, Prov.
31:15–24. Equal rights in the eyes of the Eternal are shown by the fact
that in Israel, unlike other nations of the Ancient Near East, women
have direct access to God in the cult: I Sam. 1:9–18; Lev. 12:6–8;
Prov. 7:14.

16. Greatest happiness a family of one's own, Ps. 127:3–5, 128:3–4.
Parents' duties to their children, Prov. 19:18, 22:6; duties of children
to their parents, Exod. 20:12; Deut. 5:16; Lev. 20:9; Prov. 19:26, etc.
A brother's family as much a man's care as his own, cf. the institution
of levirate marriage, by which a man has a duty to raise up sons to take
his dead brother's name: Deut. 25:5–10; Ruth 4:5–6. Concern for the
family to which one is linked by marriage, the celebrated and poignant loyalty of Ruth, Ruth 1:16, 'Intreat me not to leave thee ... for
whither thou goest, I will go; ... thy people shall be my people, and
thy God my God.' Remission of sentence on a murderer, II Sam.
14:5–11. Respect for the aged, Lev. 19:32.

17. This fact is built into the very name of the Old Testament
people, since 'Israel' is thought of as a personal name, and the community as the 'children of Israel,' *benē yisroel*, the descendants of one
patriarch; cf. 'sons of Jacob' in the same sense, Mal. 3:6. Every man's
bereaved my bereaved: Deut. 14:29; Mal. 3:5; Zech. 7:10; his poor
my poor: Deut. 15:7–11; Lev. 19:9–10. No right to deprive another of
necessities of existence, Ex. 22:26–27. Economic considerations not
alone determinative: Ex. 22:25; Deut. 15:1–11, esp. 9; nor personal
feelings: Exod. 23:4. Equal rights before the law: Exod. 23:1–3, 6–8;
Lev. 19:15, 24:22; bar on escalating revenge: Exod. 21:23–25; Lev.
24:17–21; Deut. 19:21. Equal value of all before the Eternal, regardless

of wealth or status: Prov. 17:5; 22:2; Job 31:13–15 R.S.V. ('Did not
he that made me in the womb make him?)

18. Quasi-parental status of rulers: Num. 11:12; Isa. 9:6; of any
leader or commander: Judges 5:7; II Kings 2:12, 13:14; Gen. 45:8.
Irreducible claim of each citizen to a stake in nation's wealth, Lev.
25:35–38. Resources belong not to the state but to the Eternal,
Lev. 25:23. Right of individual to trusteeship, Lev. 25:13, 28. Specialised or limited contribution entitles to benefit, Deut. 14:29. Dangers
of government power and ownership: Deut. 17:14–20; I Sam.
8:11–18.

19. One gigantic family: Gen. 3:20, 10. (the so-called 'Table of
the Nations' an attempt to comprise all the peoples of the world in a
single family tree.) Behaviour between nations, II Kings 6:22; rulers,
I Kings 20:32–33; individual members of different nations, aliens
resident in the community: Exod. 22:21, 23:9; Lev. 19:33–34 R.S.V.
('The stranger who sojourns with you shall be as the native . . . you shall
love him as thyself'); Deut. 27:19; general standards of human decency:
Gen. 19:1–13 (Sodom and Gomorrah); 20:9; Deut. 20:19–20. Laws of
personal friendship: I Sam. 20:14, 42. Man's insignificance when compared with the universe, Ps. 8:3–4 R.S.V. ('When I look at thy heavens,
the work of thy fingers, the moon and the stars, which thou hast
established, What is man, that thou art mindful of him?'). Universe not
designed merely to serve man, cf., e.g., Job 38:25–27; may be actively
hostile to him, Job 39:9–12, 41; other beings have right to be themselves:
Job 39:26–30, 40:15–24, 41:33–34; Ps. 104:24–31. Man late on scene,
Gen. 1—man last to be created; Job 38:4–21. Irrelevance of cosmos to
man: Job 38–41 *passim*. Everything has its own special relationship to
God as Father: even the ocean monsters are pets with whom he plays,
Ps. 104:26; all living things turn to him for food and life, Ps. 104:21;
Job 38:41; Ps. 145:14–16, 136:25; all created things praise him,
Ps. 148:7–13; he is especially the Father of all mankind: Isa. 63:16;
Deut. 32:11, 33:27; Hos. 11:3; Isa. 25:6–8; Pss. 89:26, 103:13,
19–22.

20. Man loses his proper scope of time: Gen. 5:3–32, vast ages in the
childhood of the world; 6:3, a limit is set on the average life of ordinary
men for their evil ways; 9:28–9 and 11:10–32, Noah the last truly
righteous man and after him a steady decline in longevity sets in;
25:7–8, Abraham's span is exceptional by the standards then prevailing;
47:9, Jacob laments that his life is short compared with that of his

fathers; 50:26, Joseph's even shorter life is that of the perfect span of a good man in Egyptian tradition; Deut. 34:7, Moses's 120 years an incredible achievement; Ps. 90:10, the general rule: seventy years normal, eighty exceptional. Man the terror of the animal kingdom: Gen. 9:2–3, this is a deliberate contrast with Gen. 1:28–9, where man is created vegetarian, and his rule over the animals is now that of a predator—or worse. The animals' 'fear and dread' of man are the direct result of human sin, and not intended by God. Man at war with the earth, Gen. 3:17–19.

21. Husband tyrannises over his wife Gen. 3:16; wife perverts her husband: Gen. 3:6, 17; I Kings 21:25 (Jezebel responsible for Ahab's crimes); 11:3. Brother murders brother, Gen. 4:1–15 (Cain, the archetypal murderer; n.b., his typical descendant, Lamech, Gen. 4:23–24, whose attitude is explicitly reversed by Christ, Matt. 18:22). Son against father, II Sam. 15:1–12 (Absalom and David); cf. Mic. 7:6. Brother defrauds brother, Gen. 25:29–34, 27. Trust a friend, not a relation, Prov. 27:10. Worker denied his fair reward: Lev. 19:13; Mal. 3:5. Any means to a quick profit: Jer. 8:10; Mic. 6:10–12; Prov. 11:1. Taking advantage of the handicapped, Deut. 27:18. Perjury: Ps. 35:11, 19–25, even to secure execution: I Kings 21:8–14; Jer. 2:34; Deut. 27:19. Property empires, Isa. 5:8–9; pauperisation and slavery, Neh. 5:1–13. Nations abandon all decency: Hab. 1:5–11; 2:9–17; Amos 1:3–2:3. General rejection of truth, etc., cf., e.g., among many passages, Isa. 5:20, 59:14–15, 5:22; Jer. 5:1; Hos. 4:1–2; Ps. 55:20–21; Amos 2:4–7.

22. Eccl. 1:2–4. Breaks will to act responsibly, Eccl. 2:17–23. No relation between virtue and happiness: Eccl. 7:15; Ps. 73:3–14; this discourages many, Job 21. Man's ability to imagine permanence, Eccl. 3:11; his actual transience: Job 9:25–26, 14:1–2; Eccl. 6:12; Ps. 90, 102:24–26, 103:15–16. No creative achievement lasts, Eccl. 2:4–11. Fate of love: Ps. 35:11–16, 55:9–14, 20–21. Good ought to be eternal; but it is not: Ps. 44:17–end; Job 9:22; Eccl. 8:10–11; Mal. 2:17. Values should be purely practical: Eccl. 2:24–25; 3:16–end, 7:16–17; making the best of transience, Eccl. 2:12–16. Awareness of the Eternal annihilates, Job 42: 1–6.

23. Death a ripe and tranquil goal, Job 5:17–26. Human personality consistently and freely willing the good, Jer. 31:33, to all other human beings, great or small, Jer. 31:34.

24. Artist or craftsman, Ex. 35:30–36:1; poet or musician: II Sam.

23:1; I Sam. 16:23; ruler or counsellor, Isa. 9:6–7; wealth: Ruth 2:1;
Gen. 13:2; and children, Job 1; building works, I Kings 22:39, 5–8.
Desire to live in peace: II Chron. 15:5; Ps. 29:11, 72:7, 122:6–7;
Isa. 26:12, 52:7, 57:19, 66:12; detestation of war: Ps. 46:9; Isa. 2:4
(Mic. 4:3). Loneliness: Gen. 2:20; Ps. 69:20. Mercy and compassion:
Ex. 2:6; I Sam. 23:21; gentleness, II Sam. 18:5; humility, Isa. 57:15;
and wisdom, Prov. 15:33. Murder: Gen. 4:1–15 and many others,
e.g., II Kings 8:7–15; war, with its attendant atrocities: Josh. 6:20;
Lam. 5:11–12; Amos 1:13; Obad. 13–14, etc.; robbery: Judges
18:22–28; Job 24:2–4, 16; violence: Gen. 49:5–7; Isa. 58:4; revenge:
I Kings 2:5–9; II Sam, 3:27; on all these cf. the poignant cry of the
professional soldier, II Sam. 2:26, R.S.V. 'Shall the sword devour for
ever? Do you not know that the end will be bitter?' Lust: II Sam.
11–12 (leading to murder, David and Bathsheba); Job 24:15; tyranny:
I Kings 11:28, 12:1–18; Eccl. 4:1–3, 5:8; Isa. 58:3; genocide, Esther
3:8–15; Unbridled self-assertion of nations: Isa. 10:7–11, 13–14;
Hab. 1:6–11; Nahum 3:19. Cowardice and treachery, Judges 15:9–13;
falsehood, II Kings 5:20–27; refusal to acknowledge unpleasant reality,
Jer. 8:11. Chaos falls on mankind, cf. the vision of Jeremiah inspired
by his nation's wickedness, in which the work of creation is reversed,
Jer. 4:23–26.

25. Knowledge of good and evil, Gen. 3:22; pleasant and unpleasant,
Isa. 7:15–16; knowledge of others: Neh. 6:12; I Kings 3:16–28; of
oneself, Prov. 14:10. Human heart ultimately a mystery: Jer. 17:9;
Prov. 16:2; final results of our acts hidden, Prov. 16:25; nature of
world only partially understood, Eccl. 11:5. He can do, but only so
much: Job 41:1–9, 14:4; care, but only ineffectually, Ps. 49:6–9.

26. Necessity of error: Ps. 51:5, 14:3.

27. Frailty and finitude, Isa. 2:22. Reduced culpability attaches to
this: Ps. 103:10–14; perhaps none at all, Jonah 4:11. 'I will do this
because I am satisfied it is right': the crux of Eve's surrender to the
serpent, Gen. 3:6; cf. Prov. 16:25. To regard oneself as the Eternal,
Ezek. 28:1–10. Humanism, Ps. 14:1 ('The fool hath said in his heart:
There is no God'). Shown up for nonsense, Dan. 4. Lunatic pride, Isa.
14:3–23, esp. 12–14.

28. Man must stand up in face of the Eternal: Job 38:3; Ezek. 2:1
R.S.V. ('Son of man, stand upon your feet, and I will speak with you!')
Passing the blame, Gen. 3:12. 'You shall' and 'you shall not' give Man
dignity: Ex. 20:1–17, cf. Deut. 5:1–21 (The Ten Commandments);

Deut. 4:5–8 (the statutes are the glory of Israel). The ways of death and life, Deut. 30:11–19.

29. Guilt against the Eternal, Ps. 51:4.

30. Not the goal envisaged by one and accepted by others, Jer. 31:34, R.S.V. No longer shall each man teach his brother. . . for they shall all know me.' This verse and the preceding one express exactly—and much better—the content of this whole paragraph.

31. Intuition of the truth, Isa. 30:19–21, 50:4. Spontaneity of heart, Ezek. 11:19–20 R.S.V. ('I will take the stony heart out of their flesh, and give them a heart of flesh'), cf. 18:31, 36:26. Learn to see the world with the mind of the Eternal, Prov. 8:12–31. The Eternal within men making them one: again, Ezek. 11:19 R.S.V. ('I will give them one heart') and Jer. 31:33–34.

32. Reward for irrational virtue, Dan. 12:2–3. Man ceases to worry, Dan. 3:16–18 R.S.V. ('Our God is able to deliver us . . . *but if not* . . . we will not serve your gods'). Living sense of partnership with the Eternal, Ex. 33:12–16 ('If thy presence will not go with me do not carry us up from here Josh. 1:5–9. The Eternals wear a human face: Gen. 18:16–33; Ezek. 1:26–27. Admit man to his friendship: Ps. 73:21–24; Gen. 5:21–24; Ex. 33:11. Deep and abiding satisfaction, Ps. 73:25–26 R.S.V. ('Whom have I in heaven but thee? And there is nothing upon earth that I desire besides thee. My flesh and my heart may fail; but God is the strength of my heart and my portion for ever').

33. Past not to affect the present, Jer. 31:34 R.S.V. (I will remember their sin no more'); Mic. 7:19. Start again with a clean sheet, Lev. 5:7–10, 11–13, 16, 18. Extreme self-torment in expiation: Mic. 6:6–67; Isa. 58:5; II Kings 6:30. Control over the future: Ps. 39:1; Jer. 7:3–5. Is there no unmerited hope? Ps. 16:9, 130:5, Lam. 3:24. Cannot the Eternal change evil into good? Gen. 50:20, R.S.V. (Joseph's tremendous words: 'As for you, you meant evil against me; but God meant it for good . . .')

34. Isa. 52:13. No guilt with regard to his fellows, Isa. 53:9. They co-operated though blind to the purpose, Isa. 53:4, 5, 6, and to the instrument, Isa. 52:14, 15, 53:1a, 2, 3. Would mean his suffering, Isa. 53:8, cf. Zech. 12:10, as he brought them into co-operation with the Eternal, Isa. 53:12b. No success or successors, Isa. 53:8b, 9. Submission to goodness and truth Isa. 53:7, prevail beyond his annihilation, Isa. 53:12a. Mankind holds up its head in pride, Isa. 53:11. Sufficient role for all for all time, Isa. 53:10b. Reconciled and joyful,

Isa. 53:1b, 5, 6b, 10a. This paragraph is an attempt to bring out from our angle of approach the meaning of perhaps the greatest single piece in the whole Old Testament.

35. Working for needs of fellow beings, Gen. 2:15. Abundance and peace: Isa. 2:2–4; Mic. 4:1–4. Rulers blessed of the ruled, Ps. 72:12–17. All creatures, Isa. 11; 65:25. Fullness of life: Jer. 31:12; Zech. 8:5, years: Isa. 65:20; Zech. 8:4, health, Ezek. 47:1–12. Knowledge: Isa. 11:9; Hab. 2:14. Love: Deut. 6:4–5; Jer. 31:1–9. Glory to the Eternal: I Chron. 29:10–13; Ps. 136, 145 ('every living thing'), 148 ('Kings of the earth and all peoples'); 117. Incorporate into eternity, Isa. 65:17. Destroy death, Isa. 25:7–8. All its members: Ps. 87:4–6; Isa. 66:22–23, 19:24–25; Zech. 8:20–22; Zeph. 3:9.

6 MAN: HIS NATURE, PREDICAMENT AND HOPE

(2) The New Testament

'Man's need and hope is . . . that the Eternal should, as it were, wear a human face.' But how could man know whether this had happened? How could he tell whether any particular man, among all the myriads that live in his past and in his present, shows him the Eternal face to face? He could only know if he saw as true a certain account of his life and condition to which *this* man brought unique illumination. He would have to plump for this account rather than others not because he saw it as demanded by some unimaginable survey of all the possible evidence about man and the world, but because, in the setting of a puzzling and difficult life in a network of relationships with men and things, and with the Eternal intruding everywhere, only this account rang true to the rich complexity of the pattern. He would accept this as the best possible guide open to him to the purpose of the Eternal himself.[1]

But this Man would not simply chime in with an already existing account which has gradually been formed in man's awareness. He would not simply be a satisfactory consummation, crowning what man already knew. He would also transform even that already existing account by setting it in the living context of his flesh and blood. If this Man really mirrors the mind of the Eternal, then all that the Eternal has ever stood for, done, intended is set in a light, which is recognisably the same of course, but new, fresh and brilliant. The portrait has been cleaned.[2]

He will do more than this. He will give a more tightly-knit unity to the features man already sees in his condition, but sees only fitfully, as they are pressed upon him by fragments of experience. Now, because of the concentration of attention on this one Man, his observable life and death, the focus is sharpened.[3] Things once disparate and isolated in the world and in man's experience are clearly in relationship with one another. There is steady continuity of purpose which nothing can change but which formerly seemed jerky and uncertain.[4]

This Man, then, offers strong satisfaction to man's desire to give unity to his experience of himself and of his world, and this is part of his attracting power. But he cannot compel man to accept this satisfaction or even the account in terms of which he offers it. Only when the action of this Man is really absorbed *as a whole* can it really begin to commend itself. It will be no good taking just certain aspects of his life and hoping to find in them anything of any special significance or use.[5] And even to take him as a whole may not suffice. Though almost any point of departure will serve, it will be a question of prolonged exposure to what this Man did and stood for, in the setting of one's whole experience. In that continual interaction, in an ever-changing pattern, this Man gradually makes his point. As this goes on in him, man might find himself driven to claims which on the face of it are improbable, at best look like poetic extravagance.[6] By this Man, what already was felt and known has been transformed, experience has received new unity, and there is a directed development of comprehension — and the Man achieved this as the human face of the Eternal. So much is unique. But the uniqueness is not Olympian, not without multitudes of lines running into the heart of man's life and experience; so that man can feel that even he himself begins to take on a new appearance.[7] In him too, because of this Man, the Eternal is wearing a human face, and his hope now seems unlimited.[8] To call this simply a solution of man's problems is unbelievably bathetic, though man will be forced to admit to those who can imagine no more that it is at least that. But it is much more glorious and positive than that: it is the beginning of free life, something wholly new to him.[9]

The clarifying role of the Man has another effect. That understanding of the condition of man which he crowns and transforms had seemed, without him, despite its magisterial strength, to be plausibly one option among others. It was, in a degree, diffuse, theoretical, speculative and open to a variety of constructions at certain points. But the Man serves to earth the speculative in the empirical,[10] to concentrate the diffuse, to eliminate possible confusion. He also serves to show that other options, apparently open to man as he makes an estimate of his condition, are wholly futile.[11] In fact, however man's condition is understood, whether in the way of which this Man is the crown, or in some other, it becomes apparent that only he, as presenting the Eternal, offers any adequate hope at all. Apart from him, not just a little hope, a chance of light, an arguable position, but no hope, no light, only sophistry.[12] By him, certain kinds of discussion about man's condition (whether he exists in any relation with the Eternal, whether the Eternal is illusory, how the Eternal's purposes can be justified in a wretched world) are not settled but shown up as mere chatter.[13] In the light of him, they seem beside the point, questions whose settlement, one way or the other, could mean little for man's true needs and could decide nothing ultimately worth deciding.

The Man who embodies the Eternal thus casts his significance over the whole sweep of human life, both historically and individually. All human societies, however remote in time or place from that in which the Man lived, are given true point because of him, because the Father is what the Son shows him to be. Because of him, none of them is wasted,[14] none without hope, however barren their achievement might seem, whatever corruption bedevilled them. Because of the Man, it is clear that the Eternal values all human life, not coldly or theoretically, but intimately and warmly. So in the individual. No detail of a man's life, however unrelated to the Eternal it may be (by accident or by design) can escape the influence of the Man: first simply because one lives in the same world, and secondly because the reality of his life, embodying the Eternal, means that nothing in a man may be discarded or rejected or evaded. This Man rubs men's noses in the realities of

their past, their present and their future.[15] Because of him there is
nothing that we can hope to get away with, just as there is no good
thing we need fear to desire. Man must first accept what he is[16]
before he dare look for the glory held in the Eternal's gift. And a
man's past will be the raw material for his glory. That which may
be truly and soberly seen as full of destruction and futility is the
only seed available for the future splendour: and because of the
Man it is amply sufficient. The Eternal can make much out of
little, everything out of nothing.[17]

If the Eternal expresses himself in the world in the life of one
member of the human family, it is not hard to see that this Man's
life is of universal significance: we are all members of the same
world, the same history. But in crucial ways, the existence of this
Man appears to make no difference whatsoever. Moreover the ways
in which he makes no difference whatsoever are those which matter
most to man and affect him most intimately, those in which he most
desperately wishes for revolutions to take place. Compared with
failure here, the ways in which he can be seen to make a difference,
even a transforming difference, seem speculative and theoretical,
refreshing to the soul but not much good for practical living. The
ways in which he makes no difference are depressingly persistent.[18]
The features of man's condition which cause him shame, anxiety
and frustration remain as they ever were. In all the ways that
affect him most deeply, man suffers exactly as he has always
suffered. The enmeshing conflicts and intractable problems can
spring up around him now just as they did in Greek tragedy or in
an ancient Egyptian text;[19] and we have no reason to believe that
the men who fought and feared in the Lascaux caves reacted to
things in their hearts in ways unknown to us. It was possible to
distinguish three aspects of man's life which turn it continually into
a 'predicament', something chafing, spoiling and to be contested.[20]
These remain as before. The existence at one time of one Man
who mirrored the Eternal brought no obvious removal of these
things and may even have intensified them by showing them in a
stronger light. If one sets out to find that removal, one finds instead
in his life only an incident in the midst of history, a man at first

out of step with the rest but in the end borne down by the predicament common to us all.[21] The apparent identity of this predicament at all times and in all societies and in each man's life accords ill with the clearly universal significance of this Man as the Eternal's act of stepping humanly into history. Is it then that the Eternal is powerless to make his points and match achievement to desire? If so, the Eternal would be admitting to being no more than those objects of hero-worship and limited, unsatisfactory aspiration with which man is always confusing him. Another possibility remains. It is that man's notion of what would constitute a solution for his problems, man's instinctive policies for alleviating his predicament do not correspond to the way taken by the Eternal. The way of the Father may be such that the life and death of this Son were wholly adequate to the case, that is, that achievement has matched desire abundantly.

What are these policies of man in the light of which the action of this Man seems to have made no difference at all to our predicament? His two chief policies are frontal attack on the immediate problem and fervent expectation of the miraculous solution. In some ways these are opposites and the failure of the one provokes him to resort to the other; and both will always fail because both serve simply to deepen man's predicament. First the frontal attack. Faced with the internal conflict caused by his desire to assert himself and his need to subordinate himself to the group, faced with his limitations of knowledge and ability which hinder the realisation of his plans, faced with black evil which erupts disturbingly, hopelessly, monotonously, man tries to rationalise and to plan.[22] The situation must be organised, the rules of the particular game must be discovered and applied. Let the rules be found and known and kept, then solutions will be in sight. And so indeed it turns out to be, at any rate in part. Order is an improvement on chaos, and it is good for man to know where he stands and what is required of him. All this is a valuable achievement, a gift worth having, and not wholly alien to the ways of the Eternal.[23] But the solution turns out never to be final, and dealing with one area shows up the disorder of the rest and rubs harshly against it, so that in some ways the predicament grows worse, demanding more plans still. Was the plan then foolish and ill-conceived? No, but it was too direct, too frontal. And worse still, it was concerned only with the problem and took no account of the Eternal in whose world man lives, and to whom the problem also belongs.[24]

Yet man will always hope much from his plans and his organising, and even when it fails and increases his frustration, hope will not die but take another, less sober turn. He makes for his alternative policy. Instead of at least facing the situation with genuine if limited realism, man develops confidence by reasoning and scheming more or less divorced from reality.[25] Something will turn up, and it can almost be proved. There will be a change of government, or a change of heart, or at least a change of weather—and this will be the turning of the tide. Let private property be abolished, or public ownership be abandoned; let a man only change his job or his wife; and, as if by a gift from heaven, a new world will have arrived. Yet Utopia never appears, and so far as it does, it never remains. The process goes on, and the predicament stays. The unrooted hope diverts attention from it and may relieve the strain, but in the end and always underneath, it presses upon man and surrounds him.

If man's instinctive policies are so fruitless, and inadequate to relieve his predicament, he finds it hard to believe that any relief is possible at all. So attached is he to his instinctive approach that when he considers what the Eternal might do for him or what difference the Eternal might make to the picture, he can only see it along those lines. The Eternal, in man's eyes, can only be man writ large.[26] But the effect of this blindness to the real ways of the Eternal, or even to the possibility that the Eternal has ways of his own, prevents man seeing what is near to his hand, prevents him seeing his predicament in the Eternal's light.[27] And if man cannot see, he cannot be relieved, and his predicament remains his predicament in the same terms as ever.

The Eternal has declared his hand in the Man who mirrors him. Then if man desires to be relieved of his predicament but can see no possibility of change in that all times and all men are alike in

suffering it, whether they live early or late, whether they attend to
the Eternal or attend instead only to the world that depends on
him, he must look more widely and deeply to see what this Man
really implies. His significance is universal in time and space for
man, simply because of his person; so much can be understood. It
is even easier to see that his influence too is wide, though not more
remarkably or surprisingly than that of certain others. But what of
his effects? What can he be said to have done that expresses man's
true nature, turns all his frustration to good, and gives substance
to his hope?

In the first place, he has given new definition to man's sight of
the Eternal and fixed attention at certain special points. Above all,
this is true of the relative weight which attaches to the elements in
the story of his life and death. For him, his death was neither an
unfortunate reverse ending useful existence nor a triumphant
gesture of defiance: it was the key episode wherein he most sharply
embodied the Eternal.[28] He showed the Eternal to be such that
alongside all other properties which he might seem to possess and
all other images under which it might be appropriate to know him,
self-abandonment in love is chief.[29] The implication is clear. Man
lives in the world in which the Eternal involves himself—and the
measure of his involvement is now disclosed. It is both willing
and unreserved. In relation to such a one, man lives his life,
willy-nilly. Obviously, if a man comes to know it, this will revolu-
tionise his attitude to everything. If *the Eternal* is reliably known
in this face, then man's relationship to the Eternal has a structure
which transforms his whole life. At the very least, his conflicts and
limitations, his frustration, and despair at guilt fall back to secondary
places. They are neither removed nor even palliated, but they are
not a final threat.[30] The Eternal, man's widest and fundamental
setting, has a character finally and utterly contradictory to all these
things; and what the Eternal is towards us is what finally matters
to us. By schooling himself in the way of the Eternal and contem-
plating the face he wears, man ought to do much better than this
'very least'. He ought to see that his predicament is not an externally
imposed weight sitting for ever upon his shoulders but is the result

of man's own failure to live appropriately with the Eternal. Because all men are at one in this, their change must also involve them all;[31] and if for one to drag his feet impedes the rest, nevertheless for one to make headway relieves and strengthens the rest. But how is 'headway' to be identified?

It will be headway to accept the Eternal as the Man who embodies him shows him to be; to know, that is, that the Eternal is neither fearsome nor remote, but, while remaining the Eternal, is open to man (to love as well as to insult and kill) and approachable to man, who can have complete confidence and venture to rise to maturity —even and especially in coming to him as to the Father. It will be headway that, because the Eternal is what he is, the base is amply laid, the setting wholly provided, for man's unfearing growth out of the condition which he can only feel as his predicament. Having accepted that base, which the self-giving love of the Eternal makes plain, he need not hanker after the old instinctive policies, feeling that without them it might be too late. His only fear will be to lose sight of the Eternal, to cease to know relationship with him. It will be headway to feel how urgent and desirable above all possible objects of desire is this acceptance of the Eternal whose love is so total. It will be headway to grasp him now in the present and to see that to defer is sheer folly.[32]

But may a man not fear that to accept the Eternal is to be swamped by him? May his individual existence, beset though it may now be, not be engulfed and annihilated by the love of such a one? Yes and no. A man will always have a master however free he thinks himself. Most masters are inescapably linked with the predicament of man: they are part of its terms, they thicken its web.[33] But the Eternal is the master who enhances a man's life unlimitedly,[34] because his love is to the utmost a generous love. It is not therefore a love which consumes and destroys but one which cherishes and acts only to enrich the beloved. It will certainly torment a man when he prefers the predicament to the hope, but the torment is part of his predicament and continuous with it;[35] it has no independent existence as a special persecution inflicted by the Eternal in an interlude of irritation.

It sounds as if the effect of the Man who embodies the Eternal upon the predicament of man is to give it a new setting, one which man might never have suspected to be the true one and one which makes possible an entirely new attitude towards it. But this is still somewhat external to the condition of man as he actually experiences it. Has this Man done more?

Of the greatest importance is the fact that through this Man, man knows that he relates to the Eternal as person to person. Here is the most important difference from his own instinctive policies of remedy. His relation to impersonal rationalisations and plans and to hoped-for revolutions is always unworthy of him as well as fruitless: unworthy of him because man can never be fulfilled in devoting himself to impersonal objects, yet at the same time needs an all-embracing objective to pursue, to give unity to his life; unworthy of him because only if he devotes himself to a personal relationship wholly open to all his aspirations, needs and possibilities can he possibly fulfil himself and pursue shared objectives alongside his fellows in the human family.

Because he relates to the Eternal as person to person, man's predicament is dealt with at the most intimate level. This can be because the Eternal has presented Himself in the Man in whose existence the predicament has already been so treated. And this Man, being one among other men in essence, though in role quite new, is able to be the seed from which much can grow.[36] Using him as the point of definition and the point of attachment, men will link themselves to the Eternal fruitfully and constructively, knowing that because of Him they can grow towards the Eternal and so towards their own freedom.

The first element in man's predicament is the conflict between his necessary assertion and expression of himself and his need to subordinate himself to the group. As attempts to resolve this conflict, no programmes of legal enactment or schemes of political organisation can provide a final solution or even a satisfactory interim solution, because they treat 'man the citizen' or 'man the economic animal' as if he were the whole man. By wrongly limiting the problem, they disastrously limit the solution. Only in relation

to the Eternal, because of the Man who reflects him, can man hope
to reconcile these conflicting aims, for here is personal relationship
with One who is also related to the rest, with the same intimacy and
thoroughness. The road to reconciliation with them must lie
through him,[37] the common point of relationship, the unifier, who
neither suppresses man nor isolates him. At this point is the only
human equality which really matters and which can then support
the richest variety in all other ways.

The conflict is intensified by man's ignorance, incapacity and
uncertainty about how to act and decide. Here too this Man opens
the way. Sometimes, in broad ways, he shows by his example what
the Eternal desires from man by way of moral conduct,[38] and
sometimes his precept adds to the picture.[39] But often man is faced
with situations where no simple reference is possible to either
example or precept. The situation is new or complex. What hope
then has man of obeying the Eternal, of returning love for love?
Little hope if for him this Man is a figure isolated in history, an
old-world example of goodness who is no longer at hand. But this
is not the case. Among those who in a continuous stream knowingly
form themselves around this Man, the Eternal through him performs an infinite series of variations upon the theme of His life and
death; and in each new set of circumstances they think his thoughts,
apply his mind to the case, his tools to the work.[40]

'Secondly, there is man's need to be rescued from his sense of
futility and injustice.'[41] Futility is not removed by any facile
assurance of life after death, for what is the point of more futility
in store in new pastures however fresh? The futility can only be
removed if man knows that the self he gradually becomes and the
other selves whom by his influence he helps to create are already
and always related to the Eternal; already, because this is the structure of things, not just 'one day' as a compensation for life at
present without meaning. The futility can only be removed if man
knows that no growth or achievement which goes into his making
is in vain but rather is built into his relationship with the Eternal
in the very moment of its coming into being. Of all this the Man
who mirrors the Eternal is the assurance; for he shows the Eternal

as wholly on the side of life and its enrichment, seeking out the positive and constructive, giving it and evoking it.[42]

Naturally therefore the Eternal makes clear in this Man that he delivers us from the guilt that haunts us. He does not do it by benevolent forgiveness. By itself this would be mere indulgence, not taking us seriously as persons who must live with themselves and cannot do it on a diet of cheering words. He does it by accepting what we are wholly and using the material, however unpromising, to make the new relationship. He leaves nothing unused, and in the end nothing untransformed.[43]

There is finally the hollowness of all man's promises of amendment of life. Any freeing from guilt about the past is clouded by the fear that the future may be no better, may even be worse. For two reasons this is no cause for despair, though ample cause for sadness. First, this Man has shown by his life that man need not be so; and the person who desires to follow the Eternal but, knowing his constitution, is fearful about his power to do so, can shed his diffidence and know that the Eternal can affect him more deeply than he imagines.[44] For this he must be ready and hopeful. He must trust the Eternal simply and directly, and not play the hardened game of hoping opposites, good and evil, simultaneously.[45] Secondly, even if the future is no better or turns to the worse, the Father's patience is never exhausted,[46] his looking to a man's future never abandoned. If this were not so, the life and death of the Man would be no accurate reflection of the Eternal.

But even in a world where man knows his condition as a predicament, a problem, he does not see it so all the time.[47] He also looks in a hopeful way and acts within it confidently and constructively. And he does this in ways that are entirely realistic and, whether he knows it or not, in line with the Eternal's will. Sometimes of course this hopefulness is foolish and not related to the facts of the world, but this is by no means always so. Yet unless the Man embodies the Eternal this reasonable hopefulness lacks adequate base and can hardly avoid the character of just making the best of things or even hoping against hope. Man feels it is more than that and acts as if it were; the Eternal, and only the Eternal, thoroughly supports this view.

Given the foundation in the will of the Eternal, man's rational hopefulness can mean wise planning and endless work for practical reform and good administering of things.[48] In full knowledge of the predicament, the sufferings and evils of man, there will be maximum effort for good. The sufferings and evils will not make the effort seem worthless or merely a desperate bid to stop the dykes, because man knows the steady will of the Eternal and sees the sufferings and evils in their true colours. They do not count against the will of the Eternal for good; they provide the conditions within which that will is accepted, grown into and explored. This will mean that a man must not greet them with peevish resentment: this will make them fruitless for good.[49] He must accept them, look them in the face, absorb them as the condition of their being the means to exploring and performing the will of the Eternal. Of course the acceptance will not be passive or complacent: that would be to identify them absolutely with the Eternal's will.[50] They are not his will; they are part of the conditions within which his will can be grown into and explored, part of the way to maturity. In acting thus, a man will act as the Man who embodied the Eternal acted, and so will find in his sufferings and evils a prime point of association with Him.[51] Here he will be glad to be associated with the Man, to have this assurance that the Eternal not only speaks but acts to meet him where he is most at sea and most vulnerable.

Man will therefore be able to combine realistic attention to all practical affairs with freedom from anxiety about them.[52] He will reach the borders of anxiety because he will show the utmost care that things are done as well as can be in line with the Eternal's will; he will frame all his relationships with the greatest desire to reflect the Eternal's love, and attend to the details of them and not just hold broad principles of sunny idealism. Always the Eternal can be trusted. He will for certain achieve his will in all his creatures, in however firm a grip 'the predicament' seems to have grasped them. Because he is the Eternal, yet is accurately reflected in the

Man who lived a life with all its details and triviality (as well as its great and striking things), everything that a man does works towards that end, positively or negatively, and is worked into the process. Nothing fails to make its contribution; but equally, nothing finally deflects the Eternal from his path.

Man thinks first of himself, even when he looks out from himself towards the Eternal; and there is no fault in this. A man is not asked to deny himself in a nihilistic sense. The life of the Man shows that man in all his depth and detail is the chief concern of the Eternal's will. But the life of the Man also points man towards his fellows and indeed makes possible adequate and fruitful relations with them, free from inevitable conflict.[53] With his necessarily limited talents, abilities and interests, a man needs his fellows in order to explore and grow into the will of the Eternal. Because of the Eternal and the Man who reflects him, he will not chafe at these limitations but accept gladly the diversity of enrichment which they open to him, both to give and to receive.[54] This enriching will not take place in all men in conscious relationship with the Eternal; nevertheless it will contribute towards the single design if it is pure giving and receiving, spontaneously done for the sake simply of the act and of the gift concerned.

It is one of man's instinctive policies, partly as a relief from his life's immediate demands, to desire now and then to know the goal of everything. But how can he know this, when he can hardly know what the day itself will bring?[55] His life is too complex, too rich to look far ahead with any assurance of accuracy. Only the Eternal can make anything of such questions or their answers, and it is for man to live as man, in relationship with the Eternal but not trying to masquerade in the Eternal's clothes. Let him in union with his fellows accept the Eternal as the setting in which he breathes and thinks. Let him love as the Eternal loves, ungraspingly but to the uttermost. Let him give and receive in freedom. And all because of the Man.

CHAPTER 6 NOTES

1. The opening paragraph refers to questions which the Bible never faces explicitly: why its account of the world and of human life should be preferred to other accounts, or indeed why any total account should be thought worth seeking at all. These are modern, not biblical questions. Nevertheless, the content of our first paragraph is not untrue to the New Testament writers, in that they present the Christian proclamation as having inherent authority. There is no attempt at water-tight demonstration, simply the affirmation that the Gospel does what it sets out to do. It is for man to find it authentic or not, to take it or leave it. The only far-reaching attempt at any kind of demonstration is in showing coherence with the message of the Old Testament if rightly regarded; but this merely shifts the question to an earlier stage. There, too, a man is faced with the choice, whether *this* way strikes him as authentic, and so convincing and authoritative, or not.

2. St. Paul is a particularly striking illustration of this point in his manner of relating the work of Christ to the Old Testament. The old religion, its law and rites, the relationship it opened for Israel with God, was satisfactory in its way (Rom. 7:12, 9:4 f.). Even ordinary human morality and reason are not useless as pointers to God (Rom. 1:19 f., 2:14–16). But, for reasons which will appear, reflection upon the significance of Christ turns these riches to tinsel (Phil 3:8 f.) and even makes them positively dangerous to man's genuine growth towards God (Rom. 7:7–11; Gal. 3:23 f.). The point is made in other ways in Hebrews, notably by the frequent use of the word *better* to describe the features of the new dispensation which results from Christ's coming (Heb. 8:6, 11:40).

3. St. Paul makes this point by his somewhat refined allegorical treatment of the incident described in Exod. 34:29–35 (see 2 Cor. 3:7–4:6). He uses the story of Moses' supernatural luminosity, received in the presence of God and so dazzling that he had to go veiled when he returned to his people, for a purpose far from the mind of the story's original writers. The veil, says St. Paul, was to prevent the Israelites from seeing that the glory gradually faded when Moses was away from the divine presence. The fading was in fact typical of the whole old covenant, which was imperfect, insufficient and transitory. Not so the new. The Christian dispensation is the exact opposite of these things,

and, in terms of the idea of supernatural light, the Christian possesses a glory of ever-increasing splendour, derived from the immediacy, stability and solidity of his relationship with Christ.

4. This is one of the chief messages of John 1:1–14, where it is expressed in terms of 'the Word'. This term has numerous literary associations in the Old Testament (Ps. 33:6; Isa. 55:10 f.) which uses it to express anthropomorphically the powerful action of God. Like a great king, God has only to speak for his commands to be carried out. But here the term is used more widely (with links connecting with the usage of the popular Greek philosophy of the author's day) to refer to God's purpose in creating and ruling the universe. The chief model for this passage is probably Gen. 1, the story of creation, where the process is described mainly by speaking of God issuing verbal orders. In that story, God simply places in the universe successive independent items (sun, moon, etc.), culminating in man himself. John, by contrast, takes pains to associate all the items with each other and with the mind of God himself. The idea of 'the Word' is the device which enables him to do this. So he starts by showing that the purpose of God has always been one and the same, eternally creative and life-giving ('In the beginning was the Word'). That purpose is indissolubly his; there is no chance of God ever altering his intentions ('the Word was God'). He goes on to show that light and life are utterly at one with this purpose and wholly expresses it (John 1:4). These terms characterise the universe as a whole and man in particular. Finally Jesus ('the Word became flesh') supremely expresses, in human terms, that single, unfailing, divine purpose. Only the coming of Christ has made this continuity and singleness of purpose clear and unmistakable. Of course, the universal New Testament motif of the fulfilment of Old Testament prophecy is a way of making the same point, sometimes rather crudely and mechanically, sometimes by showing how Christ takes up and develops theological insights adumbrated in the Old Testament.

5. The Gospels refer to Jesus receiving acclaim for inadequate reasons (Mark 8:29–33) and to his work being misinterpreted (John 6:15; Mark 6:1–6). Similarly, modern attempts to derive from the Gospels, accounts of the life of Jesus different from those of the Evangelists, tend to betray only the preconceived notions of those who make them. The evidence of the Gospels is neither sufficient in quantity nor appropriate in kind to enable this use to be made of it. In each of the Gospels, fact and interpretation are inextricably bound together.

6. Such claims began very early in the Church's life. The hymn-like passage in Phil. 2:6–11 may well be pre-pauline, but even if it was written by St. Paul it belongs at the latest to about twenty years after the death and resurrection of Jesus. Cf. also the very early identification of Jesus with the word and wisdom of God, already personified in various Old Testament passages as his agents in creation (I Cor. 1:24; 8:6).

7. The most common way of expressing this in the New Testament is to associate man, renewed in his proper relationship with God, with the status of Christ who makes that renewal possible. The believer is a son of God as Jesus is the Son, and can call God 'Father' (Rom. 8:14–17; Gal. 3:26, 4:6 f.; Heb. 3:10–13; John 15:13–15).

8. 1 John 3:1 f. In Rom. 8:18–25, man's hope is related to a changed attitude to and relationship with the material order in which he is set. His own new status in relation to God makes him look at the whole world with new eyes (cf. also the hope of a transformed universe graphically described in Rev. 21 f.). Such hope is an essential part of the divine action in Christ.

9. See Rom. 6:16–23 for play with the ideas of freedom and slavery in relation to the powers which compete for man's allegiance, God and the multifarious agencies of evil.

10. The New Testament writers saw this particularly in terms of the fulfilment of prophecy; so the Old Testament images of the word and wisdom of God, the ideas of the suffering servant of God (Isa. 52:13–53: end; 42:1–6; Ps. 22), the hope of a messiah (Ps. 2; Isa. 7:14) are all seen to have been realised in Christ. (For the word, see John 1:14 and Rev. 19:13; for wisdom, 1 Cor. 1:24; for the suffering servant, the Passion narratives in the Gospels [with Ps. 22 especially prominent behind Mark 14 f.], and passages like 1 Pet. 2:22–25; Matt. 8:17; Rom. 15:21, 10:16; Acts 8:32 f.; for the messianic hope, compare Mark 1:11 with Ps. 2:7; Matt. 1:23 with Is. 7:14).

11. 2 Cor. 3:6; Rom. 6:21; John 15:5.

12. 1 Cor. 1:18–24.

13. Titus 3:9; Col. 2:8–10.

14. Rom. 11:25 f. (St. Paul sees the issue particularly in terms of the relation of Jews and Gentiles to the promises of God, the way it affected him personally and the Church in its first days); John 12:32; 1 Cor. 12:13; Rom. 10:12. God's offer and promise are held out to all, regardless of their origins and their past; see these passages in the light of Rom. 1:20–25, 5:8.

15. Rev. 1:8 for the total sweep of God's power; Rom. 8:28–39 for the inescapable and inexhaustible quality of his love and generosity; John 3:16–19 for the connection of this with his equally inescapable judgment.

16. 1 John 1:8–10.

17. This principle applies to Christ's own work (John 12:24) and thus to the believer too (John 12:25). Cf. 1 Cor. 4:6; 5:17.

18. 2 Pet. 3:3 f.

19. See D. Winton Thomas, ed., *Documents from Old Testament Times* (Nelson 1958), p. 164:

> To whom shall I speak to-day?
> Brothers are evil,
> The companions of yesterday do not love.
> To whom shall I speak to-day?
> Hearts are rapacious,
> Every man seizes the goods of his neighbour ...
> To whom shall I speak to-day?
> Men are contented with evil,
> Goodness is neglected everywhere.

20. See p. 105.

21. And Jesus is shown accepting it at the point of deepest despair (Mark 15:34).

22. See p. 105.

23. So St. Paul, above all New Testament writers, saw the ambiguous role of law in man's moral life and in his attempt to come into a right relationship with God. In the circumstances of his own life, 'law' meant for St. Paul first and foremost the Jewish law, with its comprehensive moral and ceremonial provisions; but he also uses the term more generally to mean the whole approach to moral life by way of obedience to standards (Rom. 2:12). St. Paul saw the beneficent side of the provision of such standards for men's guidance (Rom. 7:12), but he also saw how impracticable such an approach to moral progress was (Gal. 3:21). Not only so, but it was positively harmful to man, as bringing sin to life in him (Rom. 7:7–11) and yet being powerless to help him in the moral struggle (Rom. 7:13–8:4). This had become clear because, through his conversion, Paul had become aware of a totally new way of relationship with God, that is, by association with Jesus, the messiah, the accredited emissary of God for this very purpose; a way wholly suitable

to man's personal nature, as an impersonal legal system never could be. It was also effective, in that the living power of Christ and the acceptance by God which he assured gave man the necessary setting in which moral growth could take place. Such moral growth was now not the chief end of religion, but rather the fruit of living in the true relationship with God which Christ had made available and possible. It is probable that the very terms of St. Paul's own conversion hinged upon this question and that this event revolutionised his view of law from the very start of his Christian life; for the manner of Christ's death, by crucifixion, meant that technically he was subject to a curse under the Jewish law (Deut. 21:23; cf. Gal. 3:13 f.), yet a law which condemned Jesus was clearly 'out' and had at best a preparatory role in God's providence (Gal. 3:24).

24. St. Paul saw that, while the law was part of God's beneficent provision for man, once it had been established it acquired a certain autonomy, so that obedience to it became dissociated from what was surely its chief aim: man's enjoyment of perfect fellowship with God. Therefore the law easily comes to seem independent of God, hardly derived from him at all. St. Paul saw it as given to Moses by angelic mediators and not directly by God (Gal. 3:19)—a fairly common idea in his time among both Jews and Christians, but not usually seen as depreciating the value of law as it is by St. Paul (cf. Acts 7:53; Heb. 2:2).

25. In New Testament times, the best examples are the speculative apocalyptic writings of Judaism (see C. K. Barrett, ed., *The New Testament Background: Selected Documents,* S.P.C.K. 1956, pp. 227–255); and shortly afterwards the writings of the Gnostic sects show the same characteristic, a flight from reality (see R. M. Grant, ed., *Gnosticism, an Anthology,* Collins 1961). There are signs in some New Testament books that the Church was already conscious of the need to guard against both these kinds of myth-making: (e.g. Col. 2:20–23; 1 John 4:1 f.; Luke 17:20 f.). Yet The Revelation of John and other apocalyptic passages in the New Testament, like Mark 13, seem to be part and parcel of this; and indeed, though they of course contain speculative elements and their idiom is that of Jewish apocalyptic, nevertheless their firm doctrinal base in the facts of Christ's life and death gives them an entirely different direction. They use a form of expression now difficult and uncongenial, but their main assertions could be equally well put in more philosophical theological terms. The message is not

irrevocably tied to the form in which it is expressed (see G. B. Caird, *A Commentary on the Revelation of St. John the Divine*, Black 1966, especially pp. 289–301).

26. Thus law and apocalyptic speculation were the two dominant elements in Jewish piety in the time of Jesus, while the sense of the immediacy and urgency of the relationship with God, so prominent in the old prophetic tradition, was largely lacking, except in a political sense in moments of special crisis (e.g. during the Jewish Revolt of A.D. 66–70).

27. In this light should be read the dialogues in John 3:1 ff. and 4:1–26; also the parables in Mark 4:26–31 which show the rule of God as coming to fruition under man's very nose—and yet he does not see.

28. St. John uses the word 'glorify' to mean the making clear of the true nature of God; and for him the death of Jesus is the supreme act of glorifying (cf. John 13:31). Here most clearly of all is the real nature of God made visible to man.

29. In the New Testament, theological statement is made in terms which usually have a background in the Old. The question therefore arises by what principle some Old Testament images and ideas are selected and developed in New Testament use and others frankly abandoned or transformed. The answer lies in our statement here: the Old Testament left it in some ways uncertain which of a number of different directions were to be preferred (the cynicism of Ecclesiastes or the deep faithfulness of Jeremiah). Christ determines the choice.

30. John 16:33.

31. I Cor. 15:22.

32. Jesus spoke in his parables of the urgency of receiving the Kingdom of God, accepting the fact of his rule: Matt. 12:28, 13:44–46, 25:1–13; Luke 16:1–8; Mark 1:15. He shows this to be a matter of sheer realism, almost pure common sense.

33. Man without God often believes himself to be free and in a satisfactory condition of life, but God's entry into the account shows this to be illusory. See the play along these lines in John 8:31–36, 9:39–41.

35. St. Paul speaks of the anger of God against sinful man (Rom. 1:18), but then shows that God himself provides the means of assuaging his wrath (Rom. 3:24 f.). In the 'wrath terminology', therefore, it is apparent that the anger is subordinate to the love which prompts God himself to go beyond it (Rom. 11:28 f.). God's firm desire to reconcile

man to himself outdoes his implacable hostility to all evil (Rom. 5:6–8). This is to be put alongside the cruder New Testament language about the punishment of the wicked, where it seems to be almost a self-contained end-in-itself. This impression arises partly from certain conventions of apocalyptic idiom, partly from an overriding sense of the righteousness of God, which seemed the primary datum, to be retained at high cost, certainly at the cost of ordinary humanitarian sentiment. St. Paul already, while sharing the approach of his contemporaries, shows, as we have said, important new ways of looking at some of the questions which this raises for us; though it is important to bear in mind that his questions were not precisely the same as ours. Paul's question was the same as Job's (4:17), 'Can mortal man be righteous before God?', not 'How can man's inherent dignity be maintained?' In any case, however irreconcilable these ideas seem to be with God's love for man, it is the latter which is the centre and spring of the Gospel proclamation, and this remains true for the New Testament writers, even if they do not appear to be conscious of inconsistencies so obvious to us.

36. John 12:24 f.; 2 Cor. 5:17; Col. 1:15–20.

37. The Christian community appears in the New Testament as the pioneer group, setting out the true pattern of human relationships. It enables men of all kinds to be at one (Gal. 3:28), and it acts as a home of generous love (John 15:12); but the sole basis of its existence and importance is Christ (John 10:7–9—Jesus the only entry to the flock; John 15:1–11; Rom. 12:4 f.), and God is the one source of its love (1 John 4:7–11).

38. Luke 22:51, 23:34; John 13:12–17.

39. Matt. 5–7; Luke 6:20 ff.

40. The New Testament sees the Holy Spirit as the continuing way of Christ's action through his people in ever-changing situations. See John 14:12–17, 16:13–15; 1 Cor. 2:9–16; Rom. 13:12–14.

41. See p. 106.

42. Rom. 6:3–11; John 5:24. By becoming a Christian, a man participates already in the risen life of Christ, that is, the crucial revolution in his existence has then already taken place. His death is reduced to the status of an incident ('the last enemy', 1 Cor. 15:26) in his life in Christ, and it makes sense to speak of his baptism as the 'death' which is fully significant for him: this is the point where he stakes all. More dramatically, the New Testament often sees this point in terms of the Jewish

belief in the New Age which God would one day bring into being. This New Age was seen by Judaism as the result of a world-shattering catastrophe which would bring this whole order to an end. The Church saw it as present in the coming of Christ and lavished upon that coming the theological language and imagery traditionally associated with the ushering in of the New Age. His life and death were the crucial and decisive intervention of God, and faith in him meant entry into the conditions of the New Age. 'Eternal life', a typical way of stating the Christian promise, especially in St. John's Gospel (e.g. 17:3, 3:15 f.), refers, strictly speaking, simply to the life of the New Age whose dawning was longed for and which had now appeared in the conditions of this world. This re-application of the conventional language was so remarkable that to sense it as vividly as one can is one of the best ways of feeling the full force of the early Church's account of Christ.

43. Rom. 5:1. Justification by faith signifies, in the writings of St. Paul, this acceptance which God gives to man: the transforming of man, beginning from his reception, while still in his condition of estrangement from God, into the status of sonship. Always this is seen as the transformation of man's *whole* personality: there is no sense of despair of, for example, man's bodily nature (Phil. 3:20 f.), no idea that man's difficulties might be solved by discarding the problem-causing elements in his being (cf. 1 Cor. 15:51–53). Yet there was much in the religious world of the New Testament period (pagan much more than Jewish) which could have led to such a view.

44. 2 Cor. 12:7–10; Rom. 8:31–39.

45. Matt. 6:24, 8:19–22; Mark 8:34–36.

46. Luke 15, 19:1–10, 23:34.

47. Rom. 2:10; Matt. 25:37–40. Plain human goodness, which does not look beyond the immediate act to any deeper implications that it may have, has a validity of its own, limited though it is. Similarly, presumably, plain human discovery and planning.

48. Rom. 13:1–7; I Thess. 4:9–12; 2 Thess. 3:6–13; Col. 3:18–4, 1. St. Paul, for example, is firm against any abandonment of ordinary personal and social obligations, which some of the first Christians saw as having become irrelevant. On the contrary, they receive new force (cf. 1 Pet. 2:13–17). Deep behind this in the Biblical outlook lies the idea of man's (Adam's) role as God's bailiff for ruling the created order: through Christ, the impaired sense of this stewardship is renewed (Heb. 2:5–10).

49. Rom. 8:28; 1 Pet. 2:18–25; 4:12–14.

50. In New Testament times, for Jews as well as Christians, this double attitude to evils and sufferings was often expressed by reference to quasi-personal cosmic powers, which were seen as lying behind many of the evils which afflict man, especially those for which he is in no obvious way responsible. These powers were malevolent yet not outside the orbit of God's power—they were not rival deities: neither Jews nor Christians solved (or evaded?) the problem of evil by resorting to dualism of this kind. For the early Christians, a most important way of describing Christ's work was to say that he had defeated the evil powers (e.g. Col. 2:15; Eph. 1:21) and now reigned supreme over them. To be a Christian was to enjoy the fruits of that victory. Now that this language is uncongenial at its face value, we have tried to express its significance (less colourfully) in terms of a revolutionised attitude to these evils made possible by the understanding of Christ's role and the acceptance of relationship with God through him. (See John Hick, *Evil and the God of Love*, Macmillan 1966; Austin Farrer, *Love Almighty and Ills Unlimited*, Collins 1962.)

51. 1 Pet. 2:21; Phil. 3:10; Gal. 2:20.

52. Matt. 6:25–34.

53. Mark 12:28–31.

54. 1 Cor. 12:4–31.

55. Luke 17:20 f.; Matt. 12:38–42, 6:34; Mark 13, 32.

7 THE DOCTRINE OF MAN

An Eastern Perspective

"'Every one of us has sinned against all men, and I more than any
. . . Believe me everyone is really responsible to all men for all men
and for everything. I don't know how to explain it to you, but I
feel it is so, painfully even. And how is it we went on living, getting
angry and not knowing . . . ? Yes, there was such a glory of God
all about me; birds, bees, meadows, sky, only I lived in shame and
dishonoured it all and did not notice the beauty and the glory.
"You take too many sins on yourself," Mother used to say. Mother
darling, it's for joy, not for grief I am crying. Though I can't
explain it to you, I like to humble myself before them, for I don't
know how to love them enough. If I have sinned against everyone,
yet all forgive me too, and that's heaven.'"[1] These words come
from the beginning of the 'Biographical Notes' of Father Zossima
in *The Brothers Karamazov*. They are the words of Father Zossima's
elder brother, dying of consumption at the age of nineteen, and
they have a vital significance for all that follows in the teaching of
the Russian monk.

Whatever may be our assessment of the success or failure, literary
and religious, of this section of Dostoievsky's great novel, there is
no doubt that in the mind of the writer himself these pages were of
crucial importance. Again and again in his letters he recurs to his
struggle to present the image of the saint of Russia, the truly good
man, an image which was to be based partly on what he had heard
and read of the eighteenth-century bishop and recluse, Tikhon
Zadonsky, partly on his more direct contact with the elders of the
monastery of Optino, who had so remarkable an influence in

certain circles of the nineteenth-century Russian intelligentsia. It was to be, in his intention, a portrait of a living man which would reply to all the atheism of his own time, to all the atheism of his own heart and mind. "I intend to give the answer to the whole negative side in *The Russian Monk*," he wrote; again, "If only I could depict a positive holy figure . . . Shall I, even to the smallest degree, approach my purpose?" He was vividly aware of all the pitfalls which surround the literary presentation of a character of radical goodness. ". . . Life is full of comical things and is sublime only in its innermost aspect, so, willy-nilly, for the sake of art I had to touch on the most trivial sides of the life of the monk, so as not to detract from artistic realism."[2]

It was perhaps inevitable that such an ambitious attempt to restate the whole Christian thesis in this way should not have been wholly successful. That there is something romantic, even in places sentimental, in the depiction of Father Zossima, it would be difficult altogether to deny. And yet the very fact that Dostoievsky should set out to reply to the attack on the reality of God in this way, is in itself highly important. To the problem of suffering and evil, Dostoievsky does not reply with argument or assertion, but with the depiction of a person who is able to take suffering into himself, and in doing so, transform it. It is in such a man that we see the reality of God; and to deny the existence of God is ultimately to deprive the existence of man of all value, and of all meaning. To affirm the existence of man, of a man of positive holiness, of an authentic and universal humanity, is in the mind of Dostoievsky, as of the whole Orthodox tradition, to affirm, in the profoundest way open to us, the existence and reality of God. For the holy man is the man who lives in God, and in whom God lives; who reveals by his very existence both the utter transcendence of the living God, and his terrifying nearness at the heart of man's life.

In refusing to give us a theoretical answer to the mystery of evil, and instead showing us a man and giving us a prescription for action, Dostoievsky follows the method of the Gospels, and of the greater part of Eastern theology. For even at its most technical, and it can be very technical, this is always a theology which is related to action, to the restoration of man in God. In the person of a man who lives and loves, who suffers and rejoices to the uttermost, we see both the life of man and the life of God, or rather we see the life of man restored to its true nature by being taken up into a perfect union with the life of God. In this perspective the only finally valid humanism is one which is centred upon God. For it is in God that the fulfilment of man is to be found. Apart from God, man's loves can become as destructive as his hatreds. Bound down to this world of space and time man cannot find his true destiny. A man-centred attempt to elevate man can too easily degrade him. "Concentration camps like Belsen and Dachau remain with us as symbols of the value we attach to human beings." Communism speaks of the same fact. Only when in our thought about man we are willing to open ourselves to the unlimited perspectives of the divine, can we find a true standing ground for man in all the dignity which belongs to him. "Where there is an object of worship, there cannot be a moment's doubt that life has an eternal meaning and that meaning is everywhere in the universe."[3] In the man who lives for God, we sense the presence and reality of the one to whom his life is given. As a Russian peasant boy reflected at the end of the nineteenth century on hearing of the life of a local hermit, "If he was a holy man, it means that God is here with us."[4] God is with us. In him we see that man has found his true dimensions.

It may seem curious to start an examination of the Eastern Orthodox view of man with the novels of Dostoievsky. But for very many Western readers his books provide the first glimpse of a form of Christianity which is surprisingly different from anything with which we are familiar in the West. We may not get an authoritative and fully balanced picture of the Eastern tradition in his writings, nor indeed in those of the great Russian religious thinkers of the nineteenth and twentieth century, men like Solovyov and Berdyaev. But what we do get is none the less invaluable. We find a vivid and living insight into a religious tradition very different from our own, an insight which enables us to decipher many things in the earlier history of Eastern Orthodoxy which would otherwise be obscure to us. For it is very easy to miss the specific character of the Eastern Christian tradition. The contents of its faith and worship are not so notably different from those of Western Christendom. The doctrines, the practices, the images, the structures are all there even if clothed in a different culture and language. But somehow they are all seen in a different light, and in a different perspective. They mean different things and convey different realities. And a living contact with contemporary Orthodoxy, whether in its least educated representatives, or in a great but idiosyncratic writer like Dostoievsky, can throw a flood of light back upon a whole tradition, which we tend to misread, because we assume too easily that we understand its positions and presuppositions.

Thus this specific passage of Dostoievsky will turn out to have a theological content which at first we might not suspect. We find in it a vivid expression of the sense of human solidarity, of solidarity with all men, and with all creation, which is one of the foundation stones of the Orthodox view of man. But this solidarity is not found through any loss of personal identity, rather it is found in the act of assuming personal responsibility for all things. It is by becoming a person, one who can respond to God and to his fellow men, that we rediscover our unity within the human race. This assumption of responsibility is at once a painful and a joyful thing. Painful because in a moment of vision we recognise our own blindness and cruelty, and the blindness and cruelty of all men, but joyful because at the same time we discover the reality of forgiveness which is greater than that of sin, and learn to read the experience of the first Adam who is fallen, in the light of the second Adam who is risen. For man to be man, must be transcending himself in union with God. In Christ we read the riddle of our origins.[5]

These are points which we must now examine in greater detail. First, there is the solidarity of mankind. If we had asked the Fathers of the Church whether or not they believed that the Genesis story was historically true, they might have been at a loss

K

what to reply, for neither they nor their contemporaries made the precise distinction between historical and other forms of truth which we make. Certainly they would have held that the narrative is true; but they would I think, for the most part, have held that its main significance lay in what it told us about all men, about mankind as a whole, rather than in what it told us of an original pair, historically considered. What matters is that Adam is the type of every man that is to be saved. "O Adam, what wrong did we do thee that thou didst bring the sentence of death upon us? O Adam what wrong did we do thee that thou didst not let us rejoice in paradise, the abode of God?" The reply comes in the same text, "O Adam and Eve, it is impossible for us to blame you, as it is impossible for man to blame the tongue while speaking with it. Likewise you are one with us, and we are of one kind with you."[6] It is our identity with Adam which above all is stressed.

But was not Adam before the fall, perfect and fully formed? How can our situation be compared with his? Many of the Fathers would have replied that he was as a child, innocent certainly but without experience, and hence easily tempted and misled. In some sense what was acted out in him, is acted out afresh in each one of us. Even in the narratives of Genesis, the fall is not confined to the one initial act. It is a progressive, growing thing. If for these writers the fall is considered to be something which happened in the beginning, it is none the less something which is still happening now. This is why for an Orthodox writer there is no problem in making a parallel between our position and that of Adam for 'he is one with us, and we are of one kind with him'. "Adam knew great grief when he was banished from paradise. But when he saw Abel slain by his brother Cain, Adam's grief was even heavier. His soul was heavy, and he lamented and thought, 'Peoples and nations will descend from me and multiply, and suffering will be their lot, and they will all live in enmity and seek to slay one another.' And his sorrow stretched wide as the sea, and only the soul that has come to know the Lord, and the magnitude of his love for us can understand. I too have lost grace and call with Adam; Be merciful to me, O Lord! Bestow on me the spirit of humility and love."[7]

This text from a twentieth-century writer is interesting not only from the unselfconscious way in which the writer compares his own position with that of Adam. Still more important is the statement that it is only in the light of the love of God revealed in Christ—only the soul that has come to know the Lord, and the magnitude of his love for us—that we can glimpse the grace which Adam lost, and which we have lost. Our understanding of the Gospels does not depend on our understanding of the Genesis narrative. It is the reverse which is true. And if in the first Adam we see a solidarity in sin, in the second we see a deeper reality, the solidarity in forgiveness.

This forgiveness is to be found by man through an act of repentance which involves essentially a taking of responsibility. In at least one strand of the Eastern tradition it is Adam's failure to accept responsibility for what he has done, which lies at the heart of the story. God calls on him more than once to own up, encouraging him, and seemingly baffled by the obstinacy of his creature. But Adam will not face things as they are, will not acknowledge the truth of his situation. Instead he places the responsibility on Eve, and she again, questioned by God, refuses to acknowledge her part in the act of disobedience. Had this recognition taken place, the results would have been quite different. But now that it is refused, they are expelled from paradise, and it is only then that they repent, and God in view of their repentance himself determines on his act of rescue.

It is not easy to convey how different the atmosphere is in the story of the Fall as recounted by a Byzantine theologian like Symeon the New Theologian, from the tone which it acquired in much Western theology. That something serious and tragic is taking place goes without question. Yet the attitude of God does not primarily seem to be one of anger. And there is always the feeling that God has some greater good in store, as soon as man will put aside the foolishness which prevents him recognising the facts as they are. When after the first act of disobedience, evil consequences follow, and man falls further from his first union with God, the love and care of God comes out after him, descending into the depths of mankind's separation in order to lead him on into a new and closer union with the divine. "If they had repented while they were in paradise, they would have received this paradise and nothing more. But once they had been driven out from it, for lack of repentance, and when afterwards they did repent in tears and lamentations ... God their master seeing their pains, their labours and their burdens, as well as their true repentance, willed to honour them and glorify them, and much more to make them forget all their ills; consider, I pray you, all the greatness of his love towards mankind; having descended into hell and raised them to life, he restored them not to the paradise whence they had fallen, but to the heaven of heavens."[8]

We are reminded here of the way in which Adam and Eve are depicted in the iconography of the Eastern Church, in the icon which represents at once Christ's descent into hell, and his triumph over death. In it, he is shown as drawing up our first parents from death and hell, and in them all mankind that are to be saved. "Indeed and indeed says the true God, I will never abandon them, but will reveal them as my brothers, my friends, my fathers and my mothers, my family and my inheritors. I have glorified them, and will glorify them, both in heaven above and on earth beneath and of their life, their joy and their glory there shall be no end."[9] Such is the effect of the meeting of God's love for man with the tears of man's repentance.

We come here to the second theme which is dominant in the passage of Dostoievsky from which we began, that of tears. We are often shocked and embarrassed by the floods of tears which seem to sweep through the writings of the Fathers, and which come down at least to the eighteenth century in the language of Christian prayer and devotion. In us the fountains have dried up. But these waters which are at once waters of destruction and waters of creation, can bury an old land and bring a new land to birth, making fruitful again a soil that had become sterile and stony. It is only a painful and radical breaking up and reformation of our nature which can bring us out into the fullness of human life. Undoubtedly one of the reasons why this language seems so unacceptable to us is that we associate tears exclusively with the emotions. But in fact they represent the whole of man's turning to God from sin and suffering.

It is the same with another term which is still more important in the Christian and Biblical understanding of man, the heart. Here modern psychological study has done something to restore our view of the unity of man; we can begin again to see what might be meant by an informed or understanding heart. In the thinking of the Fathers, as in the Bible, man is conceived as a body-soul unity, and the heart is the focal point not of his feeling alone, but also of his willing, his thinking and his acting. The fact that the Fathers often advocate a strict bodily asceticism does not mean that they regard the body as evil, or seek to ignore it in man's approach to God. Quite the reverse; they are convinced that man must approach God in the totality of his nature, body, mind and soul at one. In this approach to God, man's preconceived patterns of action and response have frequently to be remodelled, and it is this breaking and remaking which is involved in repentance. Certainly the emotions are involved in this. But so also are the mind and the will. Repentance demands a transformation and extension of intellectual vision no less than of sympathetic response to the needs of others. It demands acts of justice in man's social and political life, no less than new patterns of thought and feeling. For man is a unity in himself, and the process of growth into full manhood is very largely a process of the integration of his different faculties, or as the Fathers sometimes express it, a putting of the mind into the heart. This includes a perfect adjustment of body and soul, in which the body also shares in the life which is given by God.[10]

As we shall see later, this view of the crucial importance of man's body has considerable consequences in relation to man's place in the whole physical creation. For the moment we must concentrate rather on its implications for our view of man's repentance, that is of the way by which God's grace in him overcomes his suffering and sin, healing and restoring what in separation had become bound down and destroyed. St. Paul says that we are to offer our bodies to God as a living sacrifice. It is only in this way,

in the united action and suffering of the whole human person that
we are able at all to enter into and, in a measure, understand the
mystery of suffering and evil. Christ in his death upon the cross,
an offering of himself for all his brethren, has unmasked and overcome the innermost principle of evil. At this point we are all very
close to him, for all mankind is represented in the two thieves who
are crucified with him. "The wise thief is every man who suffers
for his sins as one who is responsible, and who thus shares in himself the sufferings of the Logos who suffers innocently for his
sake."[11] In this way man gains an insight into the reason for
suffering, an insight which is achieved not in word but in deed,
and in doing so finds that evil and suffering are in some way
swallowed up and even overcome. As a modern writer has said
commenting on Dostoievsky, "Ivan Karamazov, appalled by the
suffering of children, was articulate and wanted to turn his back
on experience. Alyosha, equally appalled, was inarticulate, but did
not. That is, he helped suffering children. This is perhaps the
burden of suffering—that there is only something to be done about
it. But when this is accepted not rejected, there seems to be faith—
also love."[12]

In Father Zossima, Dostoievsky makes this point with great
insistence. "If the evil doing of men moves you to indignation and
overwhelming distress, even to a desire for vengeance on the evil-
doers, shun above all things that feeling. Go at once and seek
suffering for yourself, as though you were yourself guilty of that
wrong. Accept that suffering and bear it, and your heart will find
comfort and you will understand that you too are guilty . . . When
you are left alone, pray. Love to throw yourself on the earth and kiss
it. Kiss the earth and love it with an unceasing consuming love.
Love all men, love everything . . . Water the earth with the tears of
your joy and love those tears."[13] Surely we feel there is a note of
romanticism here, a note of passionate world affirmation which
belongs to the nineteenth century, and is foreign to the severely
monastic character of the Eastern spiritual tradition. Let us take
in comparison a text from one of the great spiritual writers of
Orthodoxy. "What is a loving heart? It is a heart which is burning

with love for the whole creation, for man, for the birds, for the beasts, for the demons, for all creatures. He who has such a heart cannot see or call to mind a creature without his eyes being filled with tears by reason of the immense compassion which seizes his heart; a heart which is softened and can no longer bear to see or learn of any suffering, even the smallest pain, being inflicted upon a creature. This is why such a man never ceases to pray also for the animals, for the enemies of Truth, and for those who do him evil . . . moved by the infinite pity of those who are becoming united with God."[14] This is a love which is universal in scope. It is the love of God within the love of man, the love of man taken up into the love of God, united without any confusion or separation. Hence there is a consistent tradition in Eastern Christendom that we are to pray for the restoration of all men and all things. "I know a man who desired the salvation of his brethren so fervently that he often besought God with burning tears and with his whole heart . . . that either his brethren might be saved with him, or he might be condemned with them. For he was bound to them in the Holy Spirit, by such a bond of love that he did not even wish to enter the kingdom of heaven if to do so meant being separated from them."[15] We are far indeed from the perspective of the Western tradition which has led some even of its greatest representatives to suppose that the joys of the blessed would be enhanced by the sight of the sufferings of the condemned.

What is spoken of here in terms of a solidarity in love is the central theme of the anthropology of the Eastern Fathers; the realisation that all men are one man in Christ, the new Adam, that our life is with our brother, and that it is in the intense realisation of the unity of all men that we shall discover the true uniqueness of our own personal being. For each man is a microcosm, a world in miniature, in whom the world is summed up, and in each of the redeemed the whole Church is to be found; in each the mysteries of redemption are worked out. These are parts in which the whole is mysteriously contained, and it is through our acceptance of responsibility, our readiness to answer for ourselves and for all, that we grow into an understanding of this unity.

But it is only as man is at the same time discovering the vertical dimension of his relationship with God, that he will be able to fulfil his task of drawing together mankind, and the whole universe in which he is placed. It is only as he recognises the image of God within himself, and realises that image, that he will be able to accomplish his microcosmic function, for it is there that the true measure of his calling is to be found. Bound up with the whole universe by his physical nature, which he shares both with animate and inanimate objects, he is yet called to answer God with the yes and amen of his obedience and faithfulness. The solidarity of mankind with the whole created order, is naturally enough expressed by the writers of the Eastern tradition in terms of the physiology and cosmology of their day. For Maximus the Confessor, for example, man's dual nature, soul and body, corresponds to the duality within the universe of sensible and intelligible being. Man's unity of nature invites him to draw together the different elements of creation in a unity which does not destroy the differentiation and diversity of things, so that he may offer the praise of all things to God from whom they come. His power to do this comes in part from his natural relationship with the world. But more profoundly it depends on the way in which he transcends and goes beyond the realities in which his life is involved. Placed in space and time he yet knows a life which is beyond space and time, which brings the riches of eternity into the fragmentariness of our temporal order.

Thus in his nature man finds himself at one with the created world, while as a person he finds himself called to respond in love to his creator. In the wholeness of his being, which includes his bodily as well as his intellectual nature, his social as well as his individual life, he is called to the vision of the glory of God, in all things and beyond all things. This vision is to be glimpsed not only in prayer and adoration, but in contemplation of creation, consideration of the physical and historical realms, active service of man's life in justice and community. In all things the hidden reason is to shine through, so that all things may be seen related to the centre whence they come. Thus discerning the innermost flame of things, man is to stand as a priest before God, in and on behalf of all creation. "In his way to union with God, man in no way leaves creatures aside, but gathers together in his love the whole cosmos disordered by sin, that it may at last be transfigured by grace."[16]

In our own century we are provided with other and more dynamic concepts in which to conceive man's relations with the world in which he has evolved. But for us, no less than for Christian thinkers of earlier centuries, it is the development of man's being as personal, as one who can answer in freedom, responsibility and love which seems not only to be the fulfilment of his own destiny, but also in some mysterious way, the fulfilment of the destiny of the world in which he has grown up.

And in the thought of Eastern Christendom this call to the love and knowledge of God is at its heart a call to union with God. Man is called to become by grace what God is by nature. This call to man to become god, does not mean the destruction of his humanity. Quite the reverse; it means the fulfilment of the image, the realisation of the capacity, the achievement of the goal. In Christ we see that the complete inhabitation of man by God does not destroy but perfects our human nature. In a writer like Maximus the Confessor, this great theme is worked out without any confusion of divine and human nature, without any blurring of the distinctness and diversity of the created in its progressive union with the divine. Rather it is through a most close and intimate interpenetration at every level, that the healing process is brought about. All is by grace, the gift of God, and not by the acquisition of man. As always the theological scheme has immediate practical repercussions. The stress on humility, faith, repentance and tears, is not abandoned as we progress further into the divine life. It is seen as the way by which man is not degraded but restored, liberated from the prison of his false self, so that he may step into the clear light of his true being in God.

This need for a continual repentance, a continual renewing of the mind, a continual transcendence of achieved positions gives us a vital clue to the nature of man. "The only measure of love is that it has no measure." "We never stand still; we always advance."[17]

These words of St. John Chrysostom express a common experience and a common understanding of the life in Christ, among the Eastern Fathers. But their full implications, not only practical but theoretical have not always been seen. There is that in man which desires to make things perfect and complete, in a limited, finite sense. He wants to make things safe, and to hold them as his own, not as a gift with unconfined implications and possibilities. He wants to define himself and even, we may say, to define God. In seeking to do this he shows that he has understood neither God nor himself. The quality of openness is a quality of all true humanity; openness to a God who however intimately present in his world he may be, always goes beyond all that we can desire or think of him. It is perhaps especially necessary for us to emphasise this fact at the present time. Partly because men everywhere inside and outside the Church are in revolt against theologies which have sought to confine God within a system and to give us a complete and finished picture of the ultimate mystery of things, partly because at the same time men are everywhere conscious of the seemingly limitless possibilities of human progress in relation to the world of created things and the development of human society. A static theology is true neither to God nor man.

But the deepest root of this necessity of openness is not to be found in the created and creative possibilities of man, but in the unknowability of the riches of God. This theme of the unknowability of the God who makes himself known in Jesus, is again one of the absolute presuppositions of all patristic theology. And again it is one which needs particular emphasis in our own time. The apophatic character of Eastern theology, its preference for the way of negation in the approach to God, is a witness to the superabundant generosity of the divine being which always goes beyond what we can see or know of him, and thus, in a paradoxical way it is also a witness to the capacity for the infinite which is planted at the heart of man, created in the divine image. For the Eastern tradition which stresses with such insistence the transcendence and majesty of God, at the same time, and in the same action, underlines the dignity and calling of man his creature, called to participate in his measure in the infinite love and generosity of the creator: "Being great in this greatest of goods, in love, he became more burning than a flame of fire, being like a common father to the whole universe he imitated or rather surpassed all his predecessors in love, and by his bodily and spiritual care for his children, spending all things, possessions and thoughts and words, body and soul, for the sake of his beloved,"[18] writes St. John Chrysostom on St. Paul. It is in this universal fire of love which extends even to the bodily care of the creation, that man's nature is revealed.

In this chapter we have only been able to sketch in some of the elements in the Eastern Christian doctrine of man, and to draw attention to ways in which it differs from the commonly received traditions of the West. We have not directly asked what relevance this material has for the present day, nor have we discussed the question of how far this way of understanding the unity of man finds embodiment in the life of Eastern Orthodoxy. We cannot ignore the fact that it is a Marxist and not a Christian vision of mankind which has been the predominant influence in Russia in the last half century, and that this is an ideology which still holds a powerful attraction for large numbers of our fellow men. The working out of that love for all men, which extends even to a care for their bodies, in our own century has fallen at least as often to non-Christians as to Christians. As to the relationship between the two halves of the Christian world, it seems as though we have here another example of a strange phenomenon on which a distinguished Orthodox theologian has remarked.[19] In some way the Orthodox East seems at its heart to have a more direct and intuitive grasp of the central realities of the Christian tradition than either of the two great families of Western Christendom. But in the practical working out of the implications of that faith, while none of us have anything about which to boast, it seems as if it has been given to the West to endeavour and to accomplish more. There seems here to be something implied about complementarity of function which needs to be taken seriously by Christians of all traditions.

CHAPTER 7 NOTES

1. F. Dostoievsky, *The Brothers Karamazov*, translated by Constance Garnett, pp. 297–8.

2. Quoted in N. Gorodetsky, *St. Tikhon Zadonsky*, pp. 182–186.

3. Saunders Lewis, 'Ann Griffiths: a Literary Appreciation' in *Sobornost*, Series 5, No. 5, p. 355.

4. Archimandrite Sofrony, *The Undistorted Image,* p. 355.

5. "The old man did not serve as the model of the new man, but the new Adam of the first Adam." Nicholas Cabasilas, *La Vie en Jesus Christ,* translated by S. Broussaleux, p. 183.

6. *The Liturgy of the Ethiopian Church,* translated by M. Daoud, p. 178.

7. Archimandrite Sofrony, op cit., p. 138.

8. *Symeon Le Nouveau Théologien, Catéchéses,* edited by Mgr. B. Krivosheine, p. 404.

9. ibid., p. 406.

10. On this subject see the article of K. T. Ware, on 'The Transfiguration of the Body' in *Sacrament and Image* (ed. A. M. Allchin). It is an interesting sign of the deeply patristic nature of Anglican thinking in the nineteenth century that this idea of the participation of the body in the life of God should be found at the end of F. Paget's essay on the Sacraments in *Lux Mundi*. "His word of power even now goes forth . . ., and in the Holy Eucharist has its efficacy throughout our whole nature. It is the thought to which Hooker points in words of endless import, 'there ensueth a kind of transubstantiation in us, a true change both of body and soul, an alteration from death to life' words which rest on those of St. Irenaeus: 'As bread from the earth receiving the invocation of God is no longer common bread but the Eucharist, consisting of two things an earthly and an heavenly; so our bodies also receiving the Eucharist are no longer corruptible, having the hope of the Resurrection.' Alike in us and in the Sacrament the powers of the world to come invade the present and already move towards the victory which shall be here-after." (*Lux Mundi*, ed. C. Gore, p. 314).

11. L. Thunberg, *Microcosm and Mediator: The Theological Anthropology of Maximus the Confessor,* p. 410. I am indebted to this work at many points in this chapter.

12. N. Mosley, *Experience and Religion*, p. 96.

13. F. Dostoievsky, op. cit., p. 335.

14. St. Isaac the Syrian quoted in V. Lossky, *The Mystical Theology of the Eastern Church*, p. 111.

15. St. Symeon the New Theologian, quoted in the same work, p. 214.

16. ibid., p. 111.

17. Quoted by Fr. D. Trakatellis in an article in *Sobornost*, Series 4, No. 10, pp. 576–7. This theme of the infinite progress of man into the knowledge and love of God is particularly the theme of St. Gregory of Nyssa. Cf. the selection of his writings made by Jean Daniélon, *From Glory to Glory*.

18. ibid., p. 583.

19. See the article by Fr. Andrei Scrima in *Istina, 1958*, Nos. 3 & 4, pp. 295–328, and 443–474, but especially pp. 315–317, where he speaks of the way in which the life and teaching of the Bible and the Fathers have constantly to be 'recaptured' in the West, whereas in the East these realities are always present but often 'not assimilated, not recognised because not realised by men and women'.

8 AUGUSTINIANISM

In 1893 the Regius Professor of Ecclesiastical History at Oxford, Dr. William Bright, wrote to a young friend of his who had recently migrated from Oxford to Cambridge:

"I dare say you will profit by new points of view as presented by Cambridge life. What you have already, it appears, verified by a brief experience has been, to my mind, illustrated by the peculiar strength, and also, if one may say so, the peculiar shortcomings, of modern Cambridge theology. I hope I shall not seem to ignore the former; but while Westcott was the dominant Cambridge teacher . . . I never, for my part, could help the feeling that he was an Alexandrian Father revived under modern conditions. By some, such a phrase might be used in pure admiration; it is the fashion (for reasons which seem to me very obvious, but not at all decisive) to exalt Alexandrianism, and depress, to the lowest depths, Augustinianism. Westcott, like Clement of Alexandria, seemed to me to take his reader through a golden Platonic mist; I was not sure where I stood, or what definite objects were within view."[1]

Since then the exaltation of Alexandrianism and the depression of Augustinianism have not lessened. The reasons to which Dr. Bright referred but did not expand are no doubt to be found in the mainly optimistic view of human nature and the belief in progress which have characterised the Western world over the last hundred years. What is generally meant by Augustinianism is a particular view of the condition of human nature and of the causes of that condition which has tended to dominate Western theology. In the Anglo-Saxon world, perhaps through the influence of John

Milton's presentation, it is thought by most people to be the authentic Christian teaching. The previous chapter has shown a somewhat different approach which has an equal claim to be the Christian view, but the influence of Augustinianism has been and is still so great that an examination and assessment of it finds a proper place in this book.

Augustine was born in 354 at Thagaste in Tunisia, probably of Berber stock, of a pagan father, a civil servant of moderate means, jovial and sensual, and of a mother who has been described as 'Christian by parentage, conviction and character'. From her he early received religious teaching, but he was not baptised and by the age of sixteen only a certain devotion to the name of Jesus remained of his childhood religion. It was at this time that he took a mistress with whom he lived for the next fifteen years and who bore him a son. At the age of thirty he came to Italy and to Milan where he fell under the spell of the bishop, Ambrose, through whose preaching he began to take seriously the intellectual claims of the Catholic faith. In 386, at the age of thirty-two, and after a severe moral struggle he accepted the Christian religion and in the following year was baptised by Ambrose. Not long afterwards he returned to Africa where he became successively monk, priest and bishop. He died in 430 at the age of seventy-six.

As we shall see there is good reason to think that Augustine's views about human nature were shaped about the time of his baptism, but they were most vigorously expressed and developed in the course of the controversy with Pelagius and his followers in the years after 412. Pelagius, a Celtic monk, saw in Christianity a body of teaching and precepts which men are able to follow if they will only exert themselves. He thought of man as made by God, given free will, told what to do with it, and being able by himself to perform those commands. Such teaching seemed clean contrary to what Augustine had learned as the doctrine of the Church and to his own experience.

We may look first at what came from within him and this may for clarity be distinguished in three points. The first of these is his desire for love. Anyone who has read the *Confessions* will know

Augustine's own assertions about this, how he longed to love and to be loved. He seems always to have had around him a group of friends and we must remember that for sixteen years he led what appears to have been in fact if not in name a settled married life. He is often vilified for what he said about sexual relationships and we need Professor Burnaby's reminder that for sixteen years before his conversion Augustine led a 'normal' sexual life. Although he does take a dark view of sexual intercourse which most modern Christians would reject, he does not allow himself to be carried to the point of denying that the sexual relationship is in itself part of the goodness of the natural order. Augustine sought and enjoyed human love but, as it seemed to him, he was led to Christianity by something greater and more permanent than human love, and the most famous of all quotations from his writings is an expression of this.[2] We recall also that in another famous passage it is two loves which have built two cities.[3] For Augustine this search seems to have been involved in the love of our Lord which he had learned in childhood and which in some way remained with him throughout his wanderings in pagan philosophy, in Manicheism and in scepticism. Our Lord became for him the instrument through whom the love of God played upon him, and to that love he tried to give himself wholly. No doubt love in Augustine, as in all of us, was mixed with less divine influences, but we must allow that it is his search for and his discovery of the love of God which is the foundation and the main structure of his greatness.

In this discovery of the love of God the fact and power of sin were clearly perceived as obstacles by Augustine, first perhaps in himself, and then on reflection in the world as a whole. He became conscious of sin manifested in ignorance, in darkness, in failure to understand, but this passed into an awareness that enlightenment itself was not enough, for there was a failure to respond when enlightened. The writings of the Platonists illuminated, the expositions of Ambrose removed difficulties of the intellect, but there was still an inability to make a decision, a failure which seemed to be more than weakness, more than could properly be described in medical terms, something allied to a deep-rooted wickedness and involving responsibility. As he looked around him and back in human history this seemed to be a universal phenomenon. The assertion that there had been sinless men before Christ was attributed to Pelagius's follower, Celestius, in the charges laid against him in 412, and it became one of the points of tedious argument in the Pelagian controversy. One can understand how impatient Augustine was about it and how it seemed to him to contradict all the testimony of experience.

The third point is a sense of the overpowering grace of God. Augustine had found it impossible to follow in the power of his own unaided will what he acknowledged to be the truth. He had, as it were, been taken out of himself and this was an experience which he could never forget. But it was more than a question of the power given in the final crisis of his conversion, for looking back he thought to see God's love pressing on him at every stage. God's action, God's grace, therefore, was by no means confined to the moment of conversion and the subsequent life in Christ, but must be conceived as operative throughout a man's whole life if God chose so to make it, and without that grace it was quite impossible to come to a knowledge of the truth and to take the steps appropriate to that knowledge.

These three convictions of the love of God, the universality and wickedness of sin, the necessity and power of grace, together shaped Augustine's approach to the instruction which he received as he prepared to become a Christian. What is usually known as the Augustinian doctrine of the Fall may be considered as embracing six propositions, and not one of these is original to Augustine. All are to be found in the extant works of St. Ambrose to whose preaching Augustine listened and by whom he was baptised. The Fall doctrine therefore came to him in this form on the authority of the Church which he had accepted on his conversion. In that form he received it but added to its exposition the skill of a professional rhetorician and the power of his own experience.

The six propositions are as follows:

1. A view of evil as a *corruptio* or privation of good. This was something which Augustine shared with Ambrose though he was

influenced also by the Latin translations of Plotinus, but both saints parted company with Plotinus when they insisted on the essential goodness of that in which there is a falling away. Ambrose in his sermons on the Hexaemeron insists that God created all things essentially good and that evil is a lapse from nature. Augustine seized on this in reply to the Manicheans by whom he had himself earlier been enticed and throughout the most extreme of his anti-Pelagian writings he held to it, as he did to the assertion that man has in principle a real freedom of choice.

2. The doctrine of 'original righteousness'. Ambrose asserted more fully than any writer before him man's original state of blessedness *redopertus amictu sapientiae ac iustitiae*. Although he did not use language so extravagant as that of the Reverend Robert South[4] there is no doubt in his mind that Adam's state before the Fall was a supernatural state of grace. The body of the first man was obedient to his soul and he was potentially immortal. If he had been obedient he need not have died. This line of thought is merely developed by Augustine.

3. A literal treatment of the Fall story in Genesis 3. Here Augustine appeals explicitly to the teaching of Ambrose whom he calls 'doctor Catholicus'. This literalism is strange at first sight when we remember that it was Ambrose's *allegorical* expositions of the Old Testament which removed some of the chief difficulties that Augustine, in his pre-conversion period, had about the Bible, and it is certainly curious that in both Fathers their treatment of Genesis 3 differs so greatly from their expositions of Genesis 1 and 2. It may be that we have here an unhappy influence of St. Paul upon Augustine who saw the Fall story used in what must have seemed to him a literal way in the Pauline epistles. His curious argument with Jerome about the interpretation of the quarrel between Peter and Paul, referred to in Galatians 2:2, will remind us how sensitive Augustine was to any suggestion that what was said in those epistles should not be taken at its face value.[5]

4. The effects of the Fall are seen as two-fold—a *vitium* or hereditary moral disease, the metaphor being medical, and a *reatus* or guilt, the metaphor here being legal. Dr. N. P. Williams

suggests that these two effects together constitute the specifically
Augustinian doctrine of original sin and he commends Augustine
for clearing up the confusion which had hitherto reigned in regard
to them, but the *vitium* is clearly expounded by Ambrose who uses
the characteristically Augustinian term *concupiscentia* in relation to
it, and, as it seems to me, clearly distinguishes it from the *reatus*
on which his teaching is also quite definite and is, indeed, quoted
by Augustine.

5. The mode of transmission of these two effects of the Fall.
The *vitium* or contagion is said to be transmitted through the
ordinary processes of conception and birth, but the *reatus* is
transmitted by the fact that all men existed seminally in Adam, his
sin being in fact the sin of all, and his corruption the corruption of
all. This doctrine is based, at any rate in part, upon the mistransla-
tion of Romans 5:12 as 'in whom all sinned'. Other Western
fathers before Ambrose had said in a general way that we have all
erred in Adam because he contained us all, but Ambrose goes far
beyond that. Every man shares not only in Adam's punishment but
also in his sin, and this again is drawn out by Augustine. Tixeront
remarks on this crucial point that: "It would be difficult, I think,
to imagine a doctrine more like that of St. Augustine than this of
St. Ambrose."

6. The last point concerns the fate of the unbaptised. Ambrose
defended a doctrine of a 'baptism of blood' in the case of unbaptised
martyrs, and of a 'baptism of desire' in the case of those who,
having given proof of their very earnest desire to receive baptism,
were hindered by premature death or other unavoidable impedi-
ment from actually being baptised, but these seem to have been
concessions to the emotions roused by particular hard cases for he
says in more general terms: "Even a catechumen believes in the
Cross of the Lord Jesus, wherewith he is also signed; but unless he
be baptised in the name of the Father and of the Son and of the
Holy Ghost, he cannot receive remission of sins or imbibe the gift
of spiritual grace." He thinks it possible indeed that unbaptised
infants may be free from punishment in the next world, but can
hardly believe that they will be received into the kingdom of

heaven. The African Church was particularly sensitive on the subject of baptism and it is to be noted that the issue of infant baptism seems to have been the one which brought Celestius into conflict with the Bishop of Carthage and others before ever Augustine became involved in the Pelagian affair. If baptism is 'for the remission of sins' the questions are inescapable 'from what sins are infants freed?' and 'what happens to those who die without having been thus freed?' In the middle of the Pelagian controversy Augustine still shrank from what seemed the authorised and logical answers to these questions, as a letter to Jerome in 415 shows, but his last words on the subject, in the *opus imperfectum contra Julianum*, show him apparently accepting the full rigour of what seemed to be the orthodox position. "If the infant is not delivered from the power of darkness and remains there, why should you marvel if he who is not allowed to enter the kingdom of God is doomed to eternal fire with the devil? But if the Pelagians prepare for unbaptised infants a place of quiet and eternal life *praeter regnum Dei*, then are Christ's words false 'He that believeth and is baptised, shall be saved, but he that believeth not shall be damned'." It will be noted that he uses the unauthentic ending of St. Mark's Gospel, as do the Church of England and the Church of Rome annually as the Gospel for Ascension Day, so that again we have a problem of Scriptural testimony.

I have set out these points at some length because there is a tendency to attribute too much originality to Augustine's Fall doctrine, largely because of the long and major controversy in which he was involved. It must be remembered that having once become a Christian Augustine had the most profound respect for the authority of the Church in doctrine, and it is therefore important to understand what seemed to him to be the authoritative doctrine of the Church on the subject. It is perhaps worth remembering that he began to learn this at the age of thirty-two and that he learned it very largely from one who had not himself been baptised until the age of thirty-four, interesting examples of the effect on theology of those who approach it for the first time as mature students.

Much of what is expressed or implied in the six propositions is unacceptable to the majority of Christians today. The literal interpretation of the Fall story of Genesis 3 is rarely to be met. But if the descent of mankind from Adam and Eve is no longer believed then the doctrine of seminal identity also must be abandoned and with it the concept of original guilt, *reatus*, and consequently the belief in the damnation of unbaptised infants. Indeed the presentation of Christian belief in forensic terms at all is felt more and more to be incompatible with the spirit of the Gospels. When so much is rejected one may well ask whether any part of Augustine's teaching about the condition of man is acceptable, and it is therefore important that we should pass through the cruder and more dramatic elements in his teaching and see how he was trying to grapple with problems which, as the earlier chapters of this book suggest, are still problems. We may find that much of what he has to say about them is still worthy of our attention.

First, there is good sense in the Augustinian attitude to authority, to the Church and the Bible. The maxim 'The Church to teach, and the Bible to prove' is not, so far as I know, found in Augustine's writings but might well have been composed by him. Newman says that he learned this principle from Provost Hawkins, and it is perhaps significant that he speaks also of having learnt from the same source to anticipate that before many years were over there would be an attack made upon the books and canon of Scripture. He was then led, as he says, to have freer views on the subject of inspiration than were usual in the Church of England at the time. The whole tendency of criticism today seems to be to throw us from the sacred text on to the Church. Augustine's experience shows how necessary it is to check the current doctrine of the Church by the Scriptures, but also to look at the doctrine of the *whole* Church over long periods of its history. Authority should be a combination of revelation and of accumulated experience upon which we bring to bear the knowledge of our time. When this happens there will be conflicts but a lesson of the last hundred years is that we do well to be patient, to take long views, and to be cautious in what we say.[6]

It would be generally agreed that Augustine was right in his assertion of the fundamental goodness of Creation and in his rejection of a dualist explanation of the origin of evil. The subject has been argued endlessly in the fifteen centuries since Augustine wrote but one may take leave to doubt whether any fundamentally new argument has been added to what he said, though no doubt the substance of his reflections has been reformulated by other minds. Christians of today would hold that he was also right in his belief in the primacy of love, and in maintaining that the love of God is expressed in Jesus Christ as nowhere else in the world's history. Here some words of Dean Church are apt reinforcement.

"Here are facts and phenomena on both sides, some leading to belief, some to unbelief; and we human creatures, with our affections, our hopes and wishes and our wills, stand, as it were, solicited by either set of facts. The facts which witness to the goodness and love of God are clear and undeniable; they are not got rid of by the presence and certainty of other facts, which seem of an opposite kind; only the co-existence of the two contraries is perplexing. And then comes the question: which shall have the decisive governing influence on wills and lives? You must, by the necessity of your existence, trust one set of appearances; which will you trust? Our Lord came among us not to clear up the perplexity, but to show us which side to take."[7]

Augustine was equally right in preaching that action of God upon us which we call grace, for it is the common testimony of those who have progressed in holiness that what they are is God's doing rather than their own.

These four things, the goodness of Creation, the primacy of love, its expression in Jesus Christ, and the experience of grace are all involved in the act of faith without which the name of Christian can hardly be claimed. Doubts arise more as we move on to the question of the sinful condition of man and how this is to be described.

On his way to Christianity Augustine had passed through a phase of dualism when he threw in his lot with the Manicheans. Having become a Christian he recognised in dualism a principal enemy and he therefore laid immense emphasis on the essentially negative character of evil as a departure from good rather than as something having an independent existence of its own. This view no doubt he derived from the Platonists but he manages, as it were, to give more content to the thought of evil than a purely negative description would allow. God has created all things in a certain order, men are wholly dependent upon God, being made out of nothing, but they have the capability of refusing their ordered place and so experiencing disorder throughout their whole nature and falling away into a not-being. In a sense this is the state of every man at birth, a state of separation from God, and he has to find his place in the divine order, by responding to the love of God and becoming a member of the city which is built upon that love.

There seem here to be certain points of contact with what Dr. Lee has written earlier in this book. For example what is there said about aggression has much in common with Augustine's account of this human characteristic in the *De Civitate Dei*. Again, the 'sense of not being' to which Dr. Lee refers has obvious similarity to Augustine's account of evil. But perhaps the most important point of agreement is in the emphasis upon the unity of body and mind. Augustine is often criticised on the supposition that he never wholly emancipated himself from Manichean dualism, and it is suggested that his attitude to sex manifests this. Professor Burnaby's caveat in this respect has already been mentioned. Augustine certainly gives too much emphasis to sexual disorder as a manifestation of concupiscence, the loss of spirit's rule over flesh, but if one brings the *De Civitate Dei* into the picture alongside the anti-Manichean and anti-Pelagian writings we have aggression, the *cupiditas dominandi* set forth as another powerful aspect of concupiscence. The human mind and spirit are expressed in physical acts, but there is a certain distinction to be drawn in the effects of those acts. Speech is the physical expression of thought and so also is a blow, but speech cannot of itself kill whereas a blow can. Envy, which some would call a spiritual sin, can in the long run be devastating, but a more immediate devastation can be caused by gluttony or drunkenness which deaden the sensibilities to spiritual things. We should be cautious, therefore, in dismissing the warnings which Augustine and others give us of the need for discipline of the body. There is to be within the human personality an order which relates to the order of society and the order of the universe within which the individual lives and with which he must come to terms.

The concept of order raises the question of a man's relationship to his fellows and so leads to the problem of human solidarity. It is not necessary to accept the theory of the descent of all men from Adam and the theory of seminal identity to recognise that there is an essential solidarity in the human race. This again is acceptable to modern psychology and is supported by the witness of modern writers, some of whom are discussed elsewhere in this book, as well as by the well-known words of John Donne from which Hemingway took the title of his novel *For Whom the Bell Tolls* and Thomas Merton the title of his book *No Man is an Island*. A remarkable testimony to this thought is to be found in the fragment of autobiography of Richard Hillary, *The Last Enemy*, which is the story of a conversion from a self-centred individualism to a belief in and the determination to serve, what he calls 'common humanity'. The climax of that book is the moment at which a Cockney woman, pinned down in a bombed house with her dead child by her side, can yet have pity for Hillary as she sees the scars of his own wounds when he bends down to give her brandy to drink. In that moment of expression of her pity for him Hillary came to realise the bond which linked him at the deepest level with all mankind. Augustine's reference to the human race as a *massa*, albeit a *massa damnata*, showed a true insight.

Where Augustine erred was in developing too readily, too rhetorically and too logically the elements of the Western Fall doctrine which he had learned as a catechumen. His style betrays his training as a rhetorician. He will press on with an argument in a way which seems to be determined by the impetus of words, and having developed an argument in this way will not shrink from its consequences. There are also in him traits of brutality and unscrupulousness, seen mildly in his choice of his own successor as bishop, where he combines respect for the letter of the law with complete disregard of its spirit, and more seriously in the reasons which he gives for his change of mind about the rightness of the use of coercion in religious matters. It comes out more than once when a possible addition to the revenues of his Church is in question. It seemed to him that he could only safeguard the sovereignty of God and his sole authorship of creation by envisaging the damnation of a large part of mankind, and he does not seem to have been forced by that conclusion to any re-examination of his premises.

Nevertheless Augustine does not wholly abandon himself to determinism or to the doctrine of total depravity. T. A. Lacey expounds his thought as follows:

"I think you will capture Augustine's thought best if you picture man as exposed to a rain of influences so various as more or less to neutralise one another, leaving him in a condition of unstable equilibrium. Other creatures are entirely controlled and moved by natural impulses; they are *in ordine causarum* to such effect that an irresistible current carries them along. Their course can be calculated by an intelligence large enough and acute enough to ascertain either the real causes of their movements or the usual direction of the forces which drive them. The date of an eclipse can be accurately determined by an astronomer. The behaviour of sheep in given circumstances can be predicted pretty certainly by an experienced shepherd. If the constitution of human nature were altogether like that of other creatures, we should be able, by a more difficult and complicated calculation of the same kind, to plan beforehand the actions of men. The skill of the shepherd might be matched in the study of ethics; politics would approximate to an exact science. With sufficient knowledge it would be possible to measure the influences at work in every case, and the sum of the motives acting upon him as forces would give the direction in which a man would go. Man would not ultimately be more unstable than any other creature, animate or inanimate. But if he has a power of choice, originating in himself, he can alter the balance of forces by leaning this way or that in a manner altogether incalculable. Freedom does not imply the absence of motive; it means that to the multitude of motives pressing on the man from without is added a motive from within strong enough to determine the instability which is the result of their cross currents.[8]

The grace of God is to be regarded as the motive from within which impels a man in a certain direction though he is free to refuse. The difficulty of combining a belief in predestination to salvation, such as Augustine, following St. Paul, clearly held, with an emphasis on man's personal responsibility for choosing good and rejecting evil is an old problem. K. E. Kirk has suggested that the answer may be found in a paradox which is only tenable because we have clear instances of it in human relationships. The more perfect love is the less is it prepared to take no for an answer. It exercises upon the person loved a very curious kind of pressure which does not rob them of their freedom of will, which leaves them free to reject the advances made, and which yet can be a pressure that never ceases and even in human relationships can be all but irresistible in the long run. If this is transferred to the eternal and perfect love of God the possibility of reconciliation may be glimpsed. Love, it may be said, leaves us completely free here and now to do as we choose, to accept or reject, and so does not rob us of personal responsibility, but because it is the perfect love of God it will not take no for an answer and in the end will have its way with us whatever we do. The analogy of human experience makes this understandable, and beyond that it would seem impossible to proceed.

CHAPTER 8 NOTES

1. *Selected Letters of William Bright D.D.* ed. B. J. Kidd, 1903, p. 347
2. "Thou has made us for thyself and our heart is restless till it rest in thee." *Conf.* I, i.
3. *De Civ. Dei* XIV, xxviii.

4. "An Aristotle was but the rubbish of an Adam, and Athens but the rudiments of Paradise."

5. cf. Ep. 28:3.

6. cf. *Life and Letters of Dean Church*, ed. Mary C. Church, 1894, pp. 146, 155–7, 338.

7. ibid., pp. 275 f.

8. T. A. Lacey, *Nature, Miracle and Sin: A study of St. Augustine's conception of the natural order*, 1916, p. 60.

In our attempt to understand and evaluate the condition of man
by considering the interaction between the insights of the Christian
tradition and the pressures of our modern understanding, it seems
reasonable to consider two modern Christian thinkers who have
reacted in differing but influential and suggestive ways in their
wrestling with the problem of how man is to understand himself.
These thinkers are Bonhoeffer and Tillich. As is well known, after a
life firmly rooted in the Lutheran tradition and displaying intellectual brilliance, spiritual depth and political courage, Bonhoeffer
was imprisoned and eventually executed for his opposition to the
Nazi rulers of Germany. While in prison he seems to have been
led to reflect very deeply on his whole understanding hitherto
both of the nature of Christianity and of the nature of man, and
these reflections led him to throw out some tantalisingly brief
fragments of suggested reconstruction which have had an immense
influence because they are both penetrating in themselves and
surrounded by the attractiveness and the awesomeness of a dedi-
cated and then martyred man. Tillich, on the other hand, spent a
long life, first in Germany and then in the United States of
America, struggling to combine that which came to him from deep
insights and a wide openness into the fields of theology, philosophy and contemporary culture. What he strove to do was to work
out a systematic approach which would do justice for the time
being to the interaction of insights and pressures, and would
provide a vehicle for both an understanding and a presentation of
the Christian faith which could be seen both by believers and, at
any rate to some extent, by unbelievers, as a key to the problems

which confront modern man. It should be stressed that Tillich never claimed to be producing more than a temporary system. One of his powerfully attractive features is his awareness that the Christian is obliged to work out afresh his systematic understanding of things in the light of the new juxtaposition of pressures and insights which are produced at each stage in human history and understanding. Tillich's whole theological method was based on a belief that the Christian understanding has, of necessity, to be worked out from an interrelation between the deliverances of Christian faith and the questions posed by the state of affairs and understanding in the world. Any Christian understanding which is so arrived at has to be put to the test of subsequent dialogue and interaction so that the Christian understanding will be a constantly evolving thing. Thus he states in the second chapter of the first volume of his *Systematic Theology*, "the norm used as criterion in the present system can be stated only with reservations. In order to be a genuine norm, it must not be a private opinion of the theologian, but the expression of an encounter with the Church of the Christian message. Whether this is the case cannot be known at the present time".[1] Thus in Tillich we have someone who is concerned to work out Christian understanding as systematically as possible, while in Bonhoeffer we have a man forced to prophetic insights by the particularly searching pressures of his personal situation.

On the subject of man it seems at first sight as if the two are very considerably opposed. According to Bonhoeffer, the most important thing to be grasped and reckoned with about, at any rate, modern Western man, is that he has 'come of age'. According to Tillich what above all has to be reckoned with is that man is hindered, troubled and not infrequently crippled by anxiety-producing questions about his state and his possibilities. In *Letters and Papers from Prison* Bonhoeffer makes a direct attack on what he understands to be Tillich's approach. He says, "Of course, we now have the secularised offshoots of Christian theology, namely existentialist philosophy and the psychotherapists, who demonstrate to secure, contented and happy mankind that it is really unhappy and desperate and simply unwilling to admit that it is in a predicament about which it knows nothing, and from which only they can rescue it. Wherever there is health, strength, security, simplicity, they scent luscious fruit to gnaw at or to lay their pernicious eggs in. They set themselves to drive people to inward despair, and then the game is in their hands. That is secularised methodism. And whom does it touch? A small number of intellectuals, of degenerates, of people who regard themselves as the most important thing in the world, and who therefore like to busy themselves with themselves. The ordinary man, who spends his everyday life at work and with his family, and of course with all kinds of diversions, is not affected. He has neither the time nor the inclination to concern himself with his existential despair, or to regard his perhaps modest share of happiness as a trial, a trouble or a calamity." A little later on in the same letter he goes on, "Tillich set out to interpret the evolution of the world (against its will) in a religious sense—to give it its shape through religion. That was very brave of him, but the world unseated him and went on by itself; he, too, sought to understand the world better than it understood itself; but it felt that it was completely misunderstood, and rejected the imputation." (Letter of June 8, 1944).

The point at issue here stems from Bonhoeffer's understanding, which seems to have been almost a revelation which came to him in prison, that the Church has for a long time been seeking to get a hold on man in the alleged interests of Christianity, by stressing, exploring and even developing a false and dangerous notion of dependence. The truth is that men no longer understand themselves, nor are they to be understood, within a picture of the world and an emotive approach to the world which gives them the status of children, of beings who can neither know for themselves nor decide for themselves. When there was neither scientific knowledge nor its derived technological power, the world seemed an arbitrary and threatening mystery within which life was liable to be nasty, brutish and short. As there was no way of finding out for oneself what was the real nature of things, the interconnection of events and the patterns of possibilities, still less any chance of controlling

anything, it was necessary to take on external authority any powerful story about the way things are if there was to be any hope of
finding a meaningful and therefore liberating framework for one's
understanding of life. True knowledge thus depended on taking
things on authority from those vested with religious authority just
as any real hope of freedom and salvation depended on one's being
given or promised powers quite beyond one's own powers to close
the gaps in one's knowledge, direct the bewilderments of one's life
and put a favourable construction on the inscrutability of the powers
of the universe. For any chance of being oneself, one was dependent
on 'higher authority' given its powers, so it was (perforce) believed,
by the highest authority of all. One could be a lost child or a saved
child, but one could neither know nor decide for oneself.

But the powerful and effective exercise of the autonomy of the
human mind and spirit, of which the scientific approach is the
most characteristic example, has changed all this; except that the
Church has not recognised it, but continued to operate with both a
story and an approach which assumes childish inadequacy or can
only get a grip where such inadequacy exists or can be created.
This, or something like it, seems to have been the discovery which
Bonhoeffer came to in his prison. He always was a theologian who
was deeply concerned with the spiritual reality and depth behind
the tradition he inherited and which meant so much to him, and he
was always concerned that this reality should reach out to the actual
life of men as individuals, in community and in politics. But until
the last stage of his life he does not seem to have taken either
science or the ordinary man very seriously as posing effective
challenges to his whole understanding of Christianity. In prison
he seems to have discovered the depths and resources of 'the
ordinary man' and this led him to reflect that most men are not
agonisedly worried by the dependence questions, the ignorance
questions and the frustration questions to which Christian doctrines
and Church activities are presented as the assuaging and saving
answers.

Men have come of age, not in any sense of reaching a splendid
and fulfilling maturity, but in the sense of being liberated from

dependence on arbitrary authorities or omnipotent parent-like figures, for knowing what they wanted to know and deciding what they wanted to decide. By and large they can cope and they can cope for themselves. Further, anyone who was trying to undermine this 'adult' attitude and trick men back again into helplessness and dependence is doing something plainly unworthy of human decency and dignity and, so Bonhoeffer held, something plainly unchristian. God, as Bonhoeffer saw him in Jesus Christ, did not force himself upon the world with an authority based on the exploitation of inadequacy, nor did God stand at the point where human resources gave out, as a sort of cosmic anodyne or external barrier against the *reductio ad absurdum*. God was at the centre of life and of the world or nowhere.

What is particularly at issue here is the understanding of the dependence and independence of man. Bonhoeffer did not believe that man's coming of age meant that he had 'grown out of God'. He was not at all inclined to go in for the demythologising of either a Bultmann or a Tillich and seems to have believed to his dying day that to say that God was in Jesus was to make a statement which was much more to be taken literally and substantially than metaphorically or mythologically. He was also clear that the world needs to be understood better than it understands itself, but, he said, this does not mean 'religiously' because that goes back to false and childish dependence of an inhuman sort. Further, in his famous sketch for the restatement of Christian doctrine and the reunderstanding of the church, he mentions both Creation and the Fall. Apparently he did not think that a world come of age was either a world that had arrived or a world that was saved or fulfilled. He must surely have had some deeper reason for this optimism in a Nazi prison than mere observation of the behaviour of men. How he would have related this side of his thoughts about what might be not unfairly called the *true dependence* of men to his penetrating insight into 'coming of age' we can only guess. However, in the view of the present writer, Christians are obliged to go on from where Bonhoeffer left off. Although he has not systematised it and has left much to be worked out, he has produced a devastating critique of the frequent misuse of authority in the Christian tradition and by the Christian Church to keep men in a false bondage and dependence in the name of the Christian religion. As far as knowing for himself and deciding for himself, Western man, at any rate, has come of age and he is being rapidly joined by man everywhere.

Tillich would, I believe, agree with most of this. Certainly his whole method of correlation, of requiring the systematic theologian and, indeed, the reflective Christian, to see to it that he lives in an open and responsible dialogue, going on within himself, between the biblical and traditional material and the questions raised by life in the world shows that he assumes that no externally imposed authority inherited as such from the past can be successfully and fruitfully imposed. His method also shows that he is convinced that the world and its discoveries and its pressures have to be taken with full seriousness. But while Tillich would, I believe, agree with the general diagnosis and evaluation lying behind the notion of man's coming of age, he would not agree that man's coming of age has meant that he has no problems or is no longer a problem to himself. Here the growth of interest and activity in the fields of psychology, psychiatry and psychotherapy manifest in the bourgeois West would seem to support Tillich's thesis or at least show that Bonhoeffer's view of man and of his own understanding of himself is a partial one, however important it is. Such books as William Schofield's *Psychotherapy—the Purchase of Friendship* and Paul Halmos' *The Faith of the Counsellors* sufficiently document a wide area of unease which man has about himself and show that in many ways men do continue to reach out for some solutions to their inadequacies and uneases. The main streams in both modern literature and modern drama amply support this documentation. Thus, while Bonhoeffer's awareness of the position with regard to authority would seem to be powerfully relevant and his protest against the exploitation of human inadequacies would seem to be Christianly and humanly justified, his picture of the serenely unworried ordinary man would seem to be no more in accordance with widely observable facts than many other such generalisations.

M

What Tillich sought to do was to claim and to demonstrate a correlation between these observable areas of unease in human existence and human relationships and the insights into the human condition claimed by the Christian tradition and reflected in such admittedly mythological notions as that of the Fall. The question to be faced, in his view, is whether or not there is a 'human predicament'. "If the idealist or naturalist asserts that 'there is no human predicament', he makes an existential decision about a matter of ultimate concern."[2] This may seem to many to be an obscure and even a pompous statement, just as it may well appear pointless to discuss whether or not there is 'a human predicament'. But a wider study of Tillich's thought, rather than the peddling of a few of his characteristic phrases, is somewhat more provocative and rewarding.

His question might crudely be put 'What is the meaning of the fact that I am sometimes worried about being me or have worries in connection with my being me?' The naturalist may reply that the fact had no meaning in any other terms than those of a descriptive and causal sort provided by psychoanalysis, social psychology and the like. There is no human predicament but just the fact that numerous human beings, on numerous occasions, require certain readjustments both in the internal alignments of the component parts of their psychosomatic reality and in the external relatedness of their personalities. These adjustments are to produce a condition sufficiently balanced to prevent a person from becoming too much of a problem to himself or to others. This is all there is to it.

An idealist may also deny that there is a human predicament on the grounds that any distressing state of anxiety or unbalance, of being a problem to oneself, is really a failure of understanding. There is nothing inherent in the human situation which produces this sort of predicament. A proper understanding of the thesis/ antithesis situation would produce the liberation of synthesis or a properly trained ability to think through the confusion of phenomena to the abiding reality beyond, would lift one above the apparent predicament which is the source of distress.

Tillich's point is that these reactions, and any others, to the problem that I sometimes am to myself really presuppose and express 'an existential decision about a matter of ultimate concern'. They indicate that the exponent of this attitude and diagnosis has taken up a certain stance in his understanding of what is really involved in being himself and therefore, what is really involved in being a man. The naturalist is behaving as if he has already decided that there is nothing more in being a man than a tendency towards a homoeostatic condition which relieves from stress. The idealist is behaving as if he has already decided that natural phenomena, the processes of science, and the events of history are not really significant in being a man. To declare that in reality there is no human predicament is to make an evaluation of what is involved in being a man, is, indeed, to accept a definition of reality and therefore to at least implicitly declare where ultimate concern lies, what there is in reality to be concerned with. But is the highest possibility that is open to us either a more or less balanced adjustment to the natural phenomena which press upon us and which compose us, or an intellectual and spiritual escape to the 'ideal' which is beyond the world of happening and doing?

The truth about human reality, Tillich argues, is in fact otherwise. The ground of our being and our ultimate concern is God and the human predicament is that we are fallen. This argument, of course, arises from 'an existential decision about a matter of ultimate concern', that decision which is faith or is the decision for faith. But here the Christian is, logically and existentially, in no different situation from that of the 'naturalist' or the 'idealist'. All, in diagnosing and describing the human situation, are taking, at least by implication, decisions like the decision of faith. What needs to be exposed are the nature of the decisions involved, the grounds on which the decisions rest, and the effects of the decisions on the understanding of and the reaction to the various aspects of the human situation. The *nature* of the decision is shown by the ultimate concern which is displayed. What understanding of the ground of our being is implied? Of what sort of stuff do we understand ourselves to be and with what sort of living do we think we are occupied? The *grounds* on which the decision rests are, in the case of the Christian, those of revelation. This revelation is received through the community which is focused on the Bible as the normative record of the original creative receiving of God's word.

Unless a man receives revelation as revelation he does not, of course, hold it to be such. Tillich is perfectly well aware that he cannot by argument establish the claim of the Christian revelation to be revelation. In his systematic exposition he does not argue *for* revelation but *from* revelation. However, he does hold that men may be alerted to the possibility that revelation might be revelation by having their attention directed to questions of ultimate concern. A man, for example, may be persuaded to ask himself whether he finds it existentially satisfying or appropriate to contemplate the ground of his being, and so rest his ultimate concern, in the natural components of the universe. Such contemplation may lead him to see, hope or suspect that his ultimate concern (sc. what he is really about) takes him beyond such a ground in the direction of that of which the Biblical revelation speaks in terms of 'God'.

The other way in which a hearing may be gained for what is to be said on the basis of revelation is by showing the effects of bringing the (alleged) insights of (claimed) revelation to bear on recognisable features of human existence. This correlation of the insights arising from revelation and of the questions arising from the experiences of and reflection on the human situation is, in any case, essential to Christian understanding. That is to say that it has a necessary internal function as well as an apologetic one. For in Tillich's understanding, the existential bearing and living truth of the Christian revelation has to be discovered afresh in each age through just such correlations. The Spirit has to be allowed to bring Christian truth effectively and convincingly alive through the pressures of current questions. Christian faith does not consist of, or reside in, sets of inherited propositions.

None the less the tradition is a tradition of revelation which does prove to be the source of vital insights into the ultimate dimensions of the human situation. What is meant, then, by stating that there is indeed a human predicament and it is that we are 'fallen'? First of all it means that the Biblical myth of the Fall is to be taken seriously as a symbol pointing us towards a recognisable and actual feature of the human situation. That is to say the myth represents something that must be taken into account in evaluating and dealing with the circumstances of each human being and of all human beings.

Tillich develops his exposition of what this 'something' is by making use of the notion of *estrangement*. This is originally an Hegelian term but he finds it of particular use in building the bridge from the Biblical treatment to a modern grasping of the Biblical significance. "Man as he exists is not what he essentially is and ought to be. He is estranged from his true being. The profundity of the term 'estrangement' lies in the implication that one belongs essentially to that from which one is estranged."[3] There is a human predicament because it makes sense to say that 'man as he exists is not what he essentially is or ought to be'. The right way to understand man as he exists is to be aware that he is not what he was created to be and therefore not what he has it in him to be. This is to claim that men must be understood in a transcendent context, i.e., that you have not exhausted all that can be said about a man when you have given an exhaustive scientific description of his present state. In old-fashioned terms picked up by Tillich, his existence is at variance with his essence. His 'essence' however is not some existing Platonic 'thing' or idea or substance but consists in the fact that he is related and relatable to God and that he has the potentiality of living from beyond, and living in a manner which goes beyond, the present conditions of his existence. That is to say that the various ways in which a man is a problem to himself and men are problems to themselves are symptoms and reflections of something deeper and more universal than a mere collocation of cases of maladjustment.

Each man is living in a way and in the midst of a condition which is at variance with that which would give the true fulfilment and satisfaction to his potentialities. His potentialities are those of one created in the image of God, that is of a creature the ground of whose being lies in God who is ultimately love and personal concern. His existence is 'fallen' from this; i.e., we are not to understand all the features of actual human living which contradict or are at variance with such an understanding of man as definitive for our understanding in themselves. We have to see them in the light of the Biblical symbol of the Fall. This symbol suggests to us the possibility of finding man's true being and fulfilment in relation to the possibilities of God and not solely in the present ('fallen') actualities of human existence. "Estrangement is not a biblical term but it is implied in most of the biblical descriptions of man's predicament. It is implied in the symbols of the expulsion from paradise, in the hostility between man and nature, in the deadly hostility of brother against brother . . . estrangement is implied in Paul's statement that man perverted the image of God into that of idols, in his classical description of 'man against himself', in his vision of man's hostility against man as combined with his distorted desires."[4]

The optimistic effect of this acceptance of the Biblical insight into the true character of the human situation is well brought out by a reference of Tillich's to Freud and Nietzsche. "Libido in Freud is the unlimited desire of man to get rid of his biological, especially his sexual, tensions, and to get pleasure from the discharge of these tensions." In his elucidation of the nature of libido, Tillich believes that Freud has uncovered much about the workings of our psyche which "should not be rejected in the name of dishonest pseudo-Christian taboos against sex. Freud in his honest realism is more Christian than are these taboos. He describes, from a special angle, exactly what concupiscence means. This is especially obvious in the way Freud describes the consequences of concupiscence and its never satisfied striving. When he speaks of the 'death instinct' . . . he describes the desire to escape the pain of the never satisfied libido . . . It is the never satisfied libido in man, whether repressed or unrestrained, which produces in him the desire to get rid of himself as man. In these observations concerning man's 'discontent' with his creativity, Freud looks deeper into the human predicament than many of his followers and critics."[5]

But, Tillich argues, in the light of the Biblical insights we see that this is not all there is to say about man. "The endlessness of libido is a mark of man's estrangement. It contradicts his essential or created goodness. In man's essential relation to himself and to his world, libido is not concupiscence. It is not the infinite desire to draw the universe into one's particular existence, but it is an element of love united with the other qualities of love . . . Concupiscence, or distorted libido, wants one's own pleasure through the other being, but it does not want the other being. This is the contrast between libido as love and libido as concupiscence."[6]

What Freud diagnoses is *fallen* human nature which he takes as normative of the possibilities of human nature. Hence he has to take the negative and pessimistic line that only through repression and sublimation of the libido can man become creative. He is blinded to the possibilities of a mutual loving, inspired and sustained by the love of God, which is not an endless straining after unfulfillable desires but a desire to be united with the object of love for its own sake, with the ultimate possibility of mutual and mutually fulfilling satisfaction.

Similarly with Nietzsche's concept of 'the will to power'. This is picking up man's natural tendency for, and need of, self-affirmation in order to be himself (and is related to the part that aggression must play in the development of any human being who is to become a self). But this is understood in terms of Schopenhauer's essentially pessimistic understanding that will is the unlimited driving power in all life which produces in man the desire to come to rest through the self-negation of the will. Once again, this pessimistic outlook is the result of taking the fallen situation as normative. A will to power which is turned inward on ultimate concerns which are less than those for which men have their created potential is inevitably insatiable and unlimited so that hope of rest can lie only in self-negation. Nietzsche then tries to overcome this self-negation by declaring that we must have the courage to act out the very negativities and this leads to the destructive effects of asserting the will to power for its own sake. But neither self-negation nor destruction are the *essential* ends of will to power if we reunderstand it in the context of man's created potentiality for an ultimate concern with love. The essential activity of the will to power is the activity of the self on behalf of and in relation to other selves. As Tillich says,

"Neither libido in itself, nor the will to power in itself is characteristic of concupiscence. Both become expressions of concupiscence and estrangement when they are not united with love and therefore have no definite object."[7]

Thus the Christian is not encouraged by his belief in revelation to ignore the insights of those who have reflected deeply, probed profoundly and researched creatively into the human situation. He is obliged to take their deliverances with complete seriousness but to see them as illuminative of and illuminated by the Christian revelation. As this revelation culminates in the Gospel of Jesus Christ such correlation, if it is truly Christian, will result in a realistic optimism and an optimistic realism. The sombre realities of the human situation diagnosed by a Freud or intuited by a Nietzsche will not be denied but they will be seen in the light of the ultimate ground of our being pointed to as the God of whom the Bible speaks and known to Christians in Jesus Christ. This requires an understanding of the human predicament which takes equally seriously both its infinite potentialities in the direction of love and its actual alienation and estrangement. To be able to deal hopefully and realistically with men, including oneself, one has to be enabled to face the fact that men are alienated from themselves, from one another and from God. This is their fallen condition which is, when so understood, a potentially hopeful condition. For to be fallen is to be neither what it is intended to be nor what it is necessary to be. There is hope therefore that there may be other intentions and other possibilities than this fallen state. That this is a realistic hope is the Christian's faith for he has seen in Jesus Christ and received through the community of Jesus Christ the knowledge and faith that there is power available to set a man at one with God, his fellows and himself. Hence he has the more reason to understand the human condition as fallen, in that he has foretastes at least of the human condition as restored.

It does not seem possible that any Christian understanding of man could ignore that aspect of the Biblical pattern of which the Fall is the focusing symbol and which Tillich points to in his discussion of estrangement. Moreover, as Tillich's discussion shows, there are no empirical grounds for ignoring this, for there is more than sufficient evidence that at least one aspect of the human condition is that which can be referred to in terms of estrangement or alienation. Hence we may assume that, however valid Bonhoeffer's strictures are on the 'Christian' exploitation of human inadequacies, we cannot make use of his insights in a manner which denies the reality of that of which the Fall is a symbol. Thus I conclude that the understanding of man to which we are pointed, if we make use of the insights both of Bonhoeffer and of Tillich, is that of man as both alienated and of age.

Man remains a problem to himself and this problem, in its various aspects, is symptomatic both of his relationship with God and with his fellows and of the fact that there is something wrong with these relationships. This wrongness has to be understood in a wider variety of contexts and aspects than any one discipline or approach might suggest. There are problems about guilt, responsibility, freedom, and potentiality which must not be reduced to the insights and information of any one scientific or philosophical approach to the human situation. Such reductionism, however much it may seem to be scientifically or philosophically justified, in fact implies 'an existential decision about a matter of ultimate concern' and is by no means so straightforwardly empirical or logically simple as may be claimed. Revelation has a claim also to be heard in the overall consideration of what it is to be human. The job of the reflective Christian and, in a more specialised way, of the systematic theologian is to discover and draw attention to features of this overall situation which must not be lost sight of if the human situation is to be kept truly open to all its potentialities.

Thus, for example, Tillich argues that whatever restatements may be developed in terms of 'estrangement' "the word 'sin' cannot be overlooked. It expresses what is not implied in the term 'estrangement', namely, the personal act of turning away from that to which one belongs. ... The word 'sin' can and must be saved ... because the word has a sharpness which accusingly points to the element of personal responsibility in one's estrangement".[8] This suggestion cannot be worked out in this essay but it is cited as one more example of the lines along which it may be shown that the pattern of Biblical talk about man and his predicament provides ways of understanding factors in the human situation which can be said, on grounds of reason and observation, to be of the utmost importance in preserving and developing the truly human. The element of personal responsibility is clearly one of these. To say that man is fallen, estranged, alienated is to draw attention to the context within which personal responsibility and all the other elements of being human are to be understood and evaluated.

But to insist that man is alienated and estranged in no way requires any refusal to recognise that he is 'of age'. Immature Christians may use the language of sin and the Fall for that purpose, but the considerations urged both by Bonhoeffer and by Tillich would suggest that this is not a responsibly Christian thing to do. It is man's *false* use of his power, his self-determination, his ability to know, to respond and to choose which, according to the Biblical pattern, both is and contributes to his estrangement. It is no part of the Biblical understanding that man is not meant to have power and dominion over the things of the Universe, nor that he is not given the responsibility of knowing for himself and choosing for himself. False and forced dependence is not the Biblical ideal of man's relation to the God who is the ground of his being. As God has taken the risk of man's freedom so man has to take the risk of being responsible for himself. To this end he must 'come of age', know for himself and choose for himself. Such is his destiny. But his salvation and fulfilment lie in recognising that in choosing for himself he has put himself at variance with himself and his true and ultimate concern by fixing his choice upon himself or upon something even less worthy of his ultimate concern than himself. Man's intended potentialities are such that in grounding his being on anything less than God he puts himself at variance with the whole set and tenor of these potentialities and thus finds himself an alien to himself, in the world and before God.

CHAPTER 9 NOTES

1. P. Tillich, *Systematic Theology I*, p. 55.
2. P. Tillich, *Systematic Theology II*, p. 35.
3. ibid., pp. 51 f.
4. ibid., p. 52.
5. ibid., p. 61.
6. ibid., p. 62.
7. ibid., p. 63.
8. ibid., p. 53.

EPILOGUE

In thus examining the Christian tradition we do not wish to suggest that the Creator has laid down at some moment in the past, lines for our guidance but no longer speaks to us. Deism of that kind is far from our thoughts. We believe that God has disclosed himself in Jesus Christ, but the person of Jesus is not isolated. He stands in the midst of a history which is recorded in the Old and New Testaments and is continued in the Church, and that history is itself part of a larger history, the history of mankind. Jesus is the pattern of what is truly human and no human concern can be alien from him. In every age therefore the message of Jesus will be newly seen in relation to new circumstances, not merely seen but newly understood because new circumstances illuminate facets perceived only in part or not at all before.

The message of Jesus is not the testimony of a dead and gone figure of history. God holds us in being at every moment of our existence, and through the life-giving Spirit acts upon us. The Christian life is a response to God's action, a response made in the unique relationship which Christians call being in Christ. To the understanding and the working out of that, we bring all knowledge, for Christ is *the* truth and all truth must finally show us some aspect of him. And yet we do this, aware of our own limitations, aware of the folly of trying to make a new system of theology or world view valid for generations to come. Our theology needs, as R. W. Church wrote of Lancelot Andrewes, 'to approach man on his many sides', and to be 'instinct with the awful consciousness of our immense and hopeless ignorance of the ways and counsels of God'. The one who is at the centre both of our faith and hope eludes definition and cannot be enclosed in any human system of ideas.